The Cirrhosis Cookbook

Nourishing Recipes for Liver Health and Well-Being

Thomas Noris

Table of Contents

Introduction 1

Breakfast Recipes 5

1. Cheese and Herb Omelette 6
2. Avocado Toast with Smoked Salmon 7
3. Classic Eggs Benedict 8
4. Yogurt Parfait 9
5. Frittata 10
6. Bacon and Egg Breakfast Pizza 11
7. Breakfast Quesadilla 12
8. Scrambled Egg Muffin Cups 14
9. Avocado Toast with Egg 15
10. TikTok Egg Boil 16
11. Blueberry Pancakes 17
12. Banana Nut Muffins 18
13. Avocado Toast with Smoked Salmon 19
14. Oven Baked Omelet 20
15. Super Easy Egg Casserole 21
16. French Toast 22
17. Sheet Pan Breakfast Bake 23
18. Spanish Potato Omelet 25
19. Overnight Oats 26
20. Breakfast Egg Muffins 27
21. Quiche Lorraine 28
22. Veggie Breakfast Sandwich 29
23. Huevos Rancheros 30

24. Yummy Veggie Omelet 31
25. Overnight Blueberry French Toast 32
26. Oatmeal Soda Bread 34
27. Crispy Fried Poached Eggs 35
28. Breakfast Pork Cutlets 37
29. Sarah's Homemade Applesauce 39
30. Greek Yogurt Waffles 40

Lunch Recipes 41
31. Chicken Caesar Wrap 42
32. Delicious Egg Salad for Sandwiches 43
33. Greek Salad 44
34. Veggie and Hummus Wrap 45
35. Sloppy Joes 46
37. Veggie Wrap 47
38. Best Cream of Broccoli Soup 48
41. Avocado and Tomato Toast 49
42. Pasta Salad 50
43. Grilled Cheese Sandwich 51
44. Ukrainian Red Borscht Soup 52
45. Homemade Corn Dogs 54
46. Broccoli Cheese Soup 55
47. Caldo de Pollo 56
48. Banh Mi 57
49. Philly Steak Sandwich 59
50. Pasta Salad with Homemade Dressing 60
51. Three Bean Salad 62
52. Easy French Dip Sandwiches 63
53. Zesty Quinoa Salad 64
54. Garlic Bread Spread 65
55. Simple Pasta Salad 66

56. Egg salad ... 67
57. Pita pockets with hummus and veggies ... 68
58. Black bean and sweet potato tacos ... 69

Dinner Recipes ... 71
59. Chicken stir-fry ... 72
60. Corned Beef Roast ... 73
61. Lasagna Flatbread ... 74
62. Mississippi Chicken ... 75
63. Juicy Roasted Chicken ... 76
64. Chicken Pot Pie ... 77
65. Spaghetti Carbonara ... 79
66. Grilled Lemon Chicken with Asparagus ... 80
67. Vegetarian Chili ... 81
68. Pan-Seared Salmon with Broccoli and Quinoa ... 83
69. Vegetable Stir Fry with Tofu ... 84
70. Garlic Butter Shrimp with Zucchini Noodles ... 86
71. One Pot Chicken Alfredo ... 87
72. Turkey and Spinach Stuffed Shells ... 88
73. Beef and Broccoli Stir Fry ... 90
74. Baked Parmesan Crusted Chicken with Roasted Vegetables ... 91
75. Creamy Pesto Pasta with Chicken and Sun-Dried Tomatoes ... 93
76. Fish Tacos with Mango Salsa ... 94
77. Sausage and Vegetable Skillet ... 96
78. Lemon Butter Chicken with Asparagus ... 97
79. Slow Cooker Beef and Vegetable Soup ... 99
80. Sheet Pan Sausage and Veggie Dinner ... 100
81. Easy Meatloaf ... 101

Snacks and Dessert Recipes ... 103
82. Chinese Sweet Bun Dough ... 104

83. Creamy Whipped Feta 106
84. Air Fryer Halloumi Cheese 107
85. Apple Nachos 108
86. Hummus and Veggie Platter 109
87. Roasted Chickpeas 110
88. Feta-Spinach Puff Pastry Bites 111
89. No-Bake Energy Bites 112
90. Caprese Skewers 113
91. Cinnamon Roasted Almonds 114
92. Homemade Trail Mix 115
93. Pizza Sliders 116
94. Greek Yogurt Dip with Veggies 118
95. Avocado Toast 119
96. Antipasto Skewers 119
97. Chocolate Fudge Brownies 120
98. Rough Puff 121
99. Classic Chocolate Chip Cookies 122
100. Chocolate Chip Cookies 123
101. Strawberry Shortcake 124
102. Chocolate Mousse 125
103. Peanut Butter M&M Cookies 126
104. Peanut Butter Whipped Cream 127
105. Best Mud Pie 128
106. TikTok Brownies 130
107. Ruffled Milk Pie 131
108. Brownie Pie 133
109. Spanish Flan 136
110. Frosty Strawberry Squares 137
111. Banana Cream Pie 138

Smoothies Recipes 139
112. Strawberry Banana Smoothie 140
113. Mango Lassi Smoothie 140
114. Blueberry Kale Smoothie 141
115. Orange Creamsicle Smoothie 141
116. Mixed Berry Smoothie 142
117. Chocolate Raspberry Smoothie 142
118. Apple Cinnamon Smoothie 143
119. Tropical Mango Pineapple Smoothie 144
120. Carrot Ginger Smoothie 145
121. Watermelon Mint Smoothie 146
122. Strawberry Kiwi Smoothie 146
123. Avocado Banana Smoothie 147
124. Chocolate Cherry Smoothie 148
125. Blackberry Vanilla Smoothie 149
126. Peach Melba Smoothie 150
127. Spinach Pineapple Smoothie 151
128. Coffee Protein Smoothie 152
129. Mango Green Tea Smoothie 153
130. Blueberry Muffin Smoothie 154
131. Honeydew Lime Smoothie 155
132. Beetroot Berry Smoothie 156
133. Cherry Vanilla Smoothie 157
134. Pina Colada Smoothie 158

Conclusion 159

Introduction

Cirrhosis is a chronic liver disease characterized by the gradual replacement of healthy liver tissue with scar tissue. This serious condition can significantly impact a person's quality of life. Diet plays a crucial role in managing cirrhosis, and a cirrhosis cookbook can be an invaluable tool for individuals with this condition and their caregivers to understand the best foods to consume and avoid.

The Cirrhosis Cookbook offers information on liver-friendly foods and those that can worsen the condition. It features a variety of tasty and nutritious recipes designed to help people with cirrhosis maintain a healthy diet while enjoying their meals. Besides providing recipes, the cookbook also covers the nutritional requirements of individuals with cirrhosis, as well as meal planning and preparation tips. It may also offer insights on managing other cirrhosis-related symptoms, such as fluid retention and malnutrition.

In summary, The Cirrhosis Cookbook is an excellent resource for anyone looking to manage cirrhosis through diet and lifestyle adjustments. It offers practical and accessible guidance to help individuals with cirrhosis lead healthier and more fulfilling lives.

What is Cirrhosis

Cirrhosis occurs when healthy liver tissue is progressively replaced by scar tissue, making liver function increasingly difficult. This scarring causes functional disruption and various other issues. The liver is a vital organ responsible for removing harmful substances from the bloodstream, producing bile for digestion, and storing and releasing glucose for energy. Cirrhosis impairs these capabilities due to the liver's deterioration.

Common causes of cirrhosis include excessive alcohol consumption, hepatitis viruses, and non-alcoholic fatty liver disease (NAFLD). Autoimmune diseases, certain medications, and hereditary conditions can also contribute to cirrhosis. Symptoms may include fatigue, weakness, abdominal discomfort and swelling, jaundice (yellowing of the skin and eyes), and easy bruising and bleeding. As the disease progresses, severe complications like liver failure, portal hypertension (high blood pressure in the veins supplying the liver), and liver cancer can develop.

Cirrhosis is a life-threatening condition that requires ongoing medical care. Abstaining from alcohol and maintaining a balanced diet are healthy choices that can help manage liver disease. Medications may be prescribed to alleviate symptoms and slow disease progression.

Foods to eat and foods to avoid Managing cirrhosis involves consuming a well-balanced diet that supports liver health and helps manage disease symptoms. Here are some general guidelines on foods to eat and avoid:

Foods to eat:

- High-fiber foods like fruits, vegetables, and whole grains can help prevent constipation and promote healthy digestion.
- Lean proteins from sources like seafood, poultry, and beans are better for the liver than red meats.
- Dairy products (preferably low-fat varieties) are good sources of protein and calcium.
- Antioxidant-rich foods like berries, nuts, and seeds can protect the liver from free radical damage.
- Potassium-rich foods such as bananas, mangoes, and sweet potatoes can help maintain proper hydration levels in the body.

Foods to avoid:

- Alcohol can cause further damage to the liver
- High-sodium foods such as processed foods, canned goods, and fast food can worsen fluid retention and increase the risk of complications such as ascites (fluid buildup in the abdomen)
- Fried and fatty foods can be difficult for the liver to process and increase the risk of non-alcoholic fatty liver disease (NAFLD)
- Sugary foods and drinks can contribute to weight gain and increase the risk of diabetes, which is a risk factor for NAFLD

- Heart disease is a risk factor for non-alcoholic fatty liver disease (NAFLD), so it's best to avoid foods rich in saturated and trans fats like butter, lard, and margarine.

An individual's health and wellness objectives can best be met through the collaborative efforts of their healthcare provider and a registered dietitian.

Breakfast Recipes

1. Cheese and Herb Omelette

Ingredients:

- 2-3 eggs
- 1 tbsp. milk
- 1 tbsp. butter
- 1/4 cup grated cheese
- 1 tbsp. diced fresh herbs
- Salt and pepper to taste

Instructions:

1. Whisk the milk, eggs, salt, and pepper in a small dish until well combined.
2. When the butter is ready, it is added to a hot, nonstick frying pan. When the butter is melted and beginning to bubble, add the egg mixture.
3. Push the omelet's edges towards the center of the skillet using a spatula to let the raw egg flow into the spaces.
4. When the bottom is almost set but the top is still a little runny, sprinkle half the omelet with the shredded cheese and herbs.
5. Using the spatula, carefully fold the omelet's opposite side over the filling.
6. Once the cheese has melted and the omelet is completely formed, cook for another minute.
7. Place the hot omelet on a platter after sliding it there. Enjoy your delicious omelet with cheese and herbs!

2. Avocado Toast with Smoked Salmon

Ingredients:

- Two slices of whole-grain bread
- One ripe avocado, peeled and mashed
- 2 oz. smoked salmon
- 1 tbsp. diced fresh dill
- Salt and pepper, to taste

Instructions:

1. Toasted bread should be cooked to your preferred doneness.
2. Each piece of toast should have mashed avocado spread equally over it.
3. One oz. of smoked salmon should be spread on each piece of toast.
4. The smoked salmon should be covered with minced dill.
5. Season the meal to your liking with salt and pepper.
6. Serve right away.

3. Classic Eggs Benedict

Ingredients:

- 4 English muffins, split and toasted
- Eight slices of Canadian bacon
- Four large eggs
- 1/2 cup unsalted butter
- Three egg yolks
- 1 tbsp. fresh lemon juice
- 1/4 tsp. salt
- Pinch of cayenne pepper

Instructions:

1. In a pan, cook the Canadian bacon until just browned on both sides. Stay toasty.
2. Two inches of water should be added to a big pot, and it should be simmered.
3. Egg yolks, lemon juice, salt, and cayenne pepper should be whisked together in a shallow dish.
4. The butter should be melted over medium heat in a small skillet.
5. Whisk continuously while the egg yolk combination is placed over the simmering water until it thickens and doubles in size.
6. While continuously whisking, drizzle the melted butter in gradually until the sauce is dense and creamy.
7. By cracking the eggs into the simmering water and cooking them for 3–4 minutes, you can poach the eggs so that the whites are firm, but the yolks are still runny.
8. To make, arrange two toasted English muffin halves on a plate. A poached egg, a piece of Canadian bacon, and some hollandaise sauce are placed on each half. Serve right away.

4. Yogurt Parfait

Ingredients:

- 1 cup plain Greek yogurt
- 1/2 cup granola
- 1/2 cup mixed fresh berries (such as strawberries, blueberries, and raspberries)
- 1 tbsp. honey
- Diced nuts or seeds (such as almonds, walnuts, or chia seeds)

Instructions:

1. Combine the Greek yogurt and honey thoroughly in a small dish.
2. Layer the granola, yogurt mixture, and fresh berries in a different bowl or tumbler. Up until the top of the bowl or container, keep adding layers.
3. If preferred, garnish with extra berries and diced nuts or seeds.
4. Serve within 24 hours of refrigerating. That yogurt concoction is delicious and will keep you full for hours.

5. Frittata

Ingredients:

- Six eggs
- 1/4 cup milk
- 1/2 cup grated cheese (cheddar, feta, or parmesan work well)
- 1/2 cup diced vegetables (such as bell peppers, onions, mushrooms, and spinach)
- 1 tbsp. olive oil
- Salt and pepper to taste

Instructions:

1. Set the oven's temperature to 375°F (190°C).
2. A dish's egg, milk, salt, and pepper components should be thoroughly blended.
3. Olive oil is added to a medium-heated oven-safe pan. Add the diced veggies and cook until tender once the oil is hot.
4. After adding the grated cheese, pour the egg mixture over the skillet's veggies.
5. The frittata should be cooked on the stove for a few minutes or until the center is barely set but the edges are firm.
6. Bake the skillet for 10 to 15 minutes until the frittata has set, and the cheese is melted and golden.
7. The frittata
8. must rest for a while after being removed from the oven.
9. After cutting the frittata
10. into segments, serve it warm or at room temperature. Have a delicious and satisfying frittata!

6. Bacon and Egg Breakfast Pizza

Ingredients:

- 1 lb pizza dough
- 1/2 cup tomato sauce
- 1 cup shredded mozzarella cheese
- Four slices bacon, cooked and crumbled
- Four large eggs
- Salt and pepper, to taste
- 1 tbsp. Diced fresh parsley

Instructions:

1. Set the oven's temperature to 425°F (220°C).
2. The pizza dough is rolled out onto a lightly floured surface into a 12-inch circle.
3. Pizza dough should be transferred to a baking tray covered with parchment paper.
4. With a 1-inch border around the sides, cover the pizza dough with tomato sauce.
5. Over the tomato sauce, top with the crumbled bacon and grated mozzarella cheese.
6. Spread the eggs equally apart across the pizza.
7. Season the eggs to taste with salt and pepper.
8. If you want the crust to be golden and the eggs to be done to your taste, bake the pizza for 12–15 minutes.
9. If preferred, scatter the parsley on top of the pizza.
10. Serve hot breakfast pizza that has been cut into pieces.

7. Breakfast Quesadilla

Ingredients:

- Two large flour tortillas
- Four large eggs, beaten
- 1/2 cup cooked and crumbled breakfast sausage
- 1/2 cup shredded cheddar cheese
- 1/4 cup diced green onions
- Salt and pepper, to taste
- 1 tbsp. vegetable oil

Instructions:

1. A big skillet should be heated to medium.
2. In a bowl, whisk the eggs and season them with salt and pepper.
3. For about 3 to 4 minutes, add the breakfast meat to the skillet and heat until it is browned and crumbled.
4. Add the beaten eggs to the skillet once fully cooked, and scramble them for three to four minutes.
5. The eggs and sausage should be transferred to a dish after turning off the heat in the skillet.
6. Make use of paper cloth to clean the skillet.
7. A flour tortilla should be placed in the skillet with half the shredded cheddar cheese on one side.
8. Cover the meat and scrambled eggs with half of the cheese.
9. Over the eggs and pork, scatter half of the green onions that have been diced.
10. To form a half-moon, fold the remaining tortilla over the center.

11. Repeat with the remaining components and tortillas.
12. While the pan is heating up over medium heat, add the vegetable oil.
13. To make sure the cheese melts and the tortillas stay crisp, cook the quesadillas for about 3 minutes on each side.
14. To serve, take the quesadillas out of the skillet and cut them into pieces.

8. Scrambled Egg Muffin Cups

Ingredients:

- ½ lb bulk pork sausage
- 12 eggs
- ½ cup diced onion
- ½ cup diced green bell pepper, or to taste
- ½ tsp. salt
- ¼ tsp. ground black pepper
- ¼ tsp. garlic powder
- ½ cup shredded Cheddar cheese

Instructions:

1. Get the oven to a temperature of 350 degrees F. 175 degrees C.. Twelve muffin tins should be lightly greased or lined with paper inserts.
2. The heat in a large skillet should be set to medium. Sausage is added and cooked for 10 to 15 minutes until it is crumbly, uniformly browned, and no longer pink. Remove the oil.
3. In a large dish, beat the eggs. Mix in the garlic powder, salt, pepper, onion, and green pepper. Cheese and pork should be combined. Into the prepped muffin cups, spoon.
4. Wait 20–25 minutes, or until a knife inserted near the dish's center comes out clean, before serving.

9. Avocado Toast with Egg

Ingredients:

- 1-2 slices of bread
- One avocado
- One egg
- Salt and pepper to taste

Toppings:

- Sliced tomatoes, red pepper flakes, diced herbs

Instructions:

1. Toasted bread should be cooked to your preferred doneness.
2. Cut the avocado in half during the toasting of the bread and remove the pit. Take the meat out and mash it with a fork in a bowl.
3. Fry an egg until it reaches the required doneness.
4. Toss the mashed avocado with salt and pepper and spread it on the bread.
5. Add the cooked egg on top and any extra garnishes you prefer.

10. TikTok Egg Boil

Ingredients:

- Four large eggs
- 2 tbsp. unsalted butter
- ¼ cup minced white onion
- One clove of garlic, minced
- 1 tbsp. hot sauce
- 1 tsp. seafood seasoning
- ½ cup low-sodium chicken broth or vegetable broth, or water
- 1 tbsp. fresh lemon juice
- 2 tbsp. Finely diced fresh parsley, plus more for garnish

Instructions:

1. Place a small pot with water halfway on high heat and come to a boil. Add the eggs carefully once the water begins to boil. Remove from heat after 1 minute. Put in a dish full of ice and set aside for three minutes to cool.
2. Butter should be melted in a small pan over low heat. Cook the onion for three minutes at a low simmer, or until it is soft and fragrant. Cook the garlic for two minutes, stirring occasionally, until it is golden and fragrant. Old Bay seasoning, hot sauce, and chicken broth are all combined and cooked for 4 minutes or until barely reduced. Lemon juice and parsley are added after the pan is removed from the heat.
3. Put the peeled eggs in a serving dish. Add sauce to the eggs and top with the leftover parsley for decoration.

11. Blueberry Pancakes

Ingredients:

- 1 cup flour
- 1 tbsp. sugar
- 1 tsp. baking powder
- 1/2 tsp. baking soda
- 1/4 tsp. salt
- One egg
- 1 cup milk
- 1/2 cup blueberries
- Butter for cooking

Instructions:

1. Mix the flour, sugar, baking soda, baking powder, and salt in a sizable dish.
2. Milk and egg should be mixed in a separate bowl.
3. Mix the dry ingredients just until combined after adding the wet components.
4. Add the blueberries and stir.
5. Melt some butter in a saucepan while it's heated to medium heat.
6. For each pancake, pour approximately 1/4 cup of batter into the skillet.
7. Wait for the bubbles to appear on the surface, then flip and cook until the other side is browned.
8. Serve with honey and butter.

12. Banana Nut Muffins

Ingredients:

- 1 1/2 cups flour
- 1 tsp. baking soda
- 1/4 tsp. salt
- 1/2 cup butter, softened
- 3/4 cup sugar
- Two eggs
- 1 tsp. vanilla extract
- Three ripe bananas, mashed
- 1/2 cup diced nuts

Instructions:

1. Paper liners should cover a muffin pan as the oven is preheated to 350°F (180°C).
2. Mix the baking powder, salt, and flour through a sieve into a small to the medium dish.
3. In a separate bowl, beat the butter and sugar until light and fluffy.
4. The eggs should be mixed in one at a time. Next, beat in the vanilla essence and mashed bananas.
5. Mix the dry components just until combined after adding them to the wet ones.
6. Add the diced almonds and stir.
7. Put about two-thirds of the batter into each prepared muffin tin cup.
8. A toothpick put into the center of a muffin should come out clean after baking for 18 to 20 minutes.
9. After a few minutes, transfer the muffins to a wire rack to cool completely.

13. Avocado Toast with Smoked Salmon

Ingredients:

- Two slices of whole-grain bread
- One ripe avocado, peeled and mashed
- 2 oz. smoked salmon
- 1 tbsp. diced fresh dill
- Salt and pepper, to taste

Instructions:

1. Toasted bread should be cooked to your preferred doneness.
2. Each piece of toast should have mashed avocado spread equally over it.
3. One oz. of smoked salmon should be spread on each piece of toast.
4. The smoked salmon should be covered with minced dill.
5. Put salt and pepper on the food to taste.
6. Serve right away.

14. Oven Baked Omelet

Ingredients:

- 1 tsp. butter
- Nine large eggs
- ½ cup sour cream
- ½ cup milk
- 1 tsp. salt
- Two green onions, diced
- ¼ cup shredded Cheddar cheese

Instructions:

1. Crank up the heat to 350 degrees F. temperature of 175 degrees C. A square baking dish, 8 inches by 8 inches, should be greased with butter.
2. In a dish, stir together the salt, milk, sour cream, and eggs. Add green scallions and stir. Fill the baking dish with the ingredients.
3. Bake it for 25 to 30 minutes, or until it reaches the desired consistency. Bake for two or three minutes with the cheese on top of the eggs to melt the cheese.

15. Super Easy Egg Casserole

Ingredients:

- Six eggs, whisked
- 1 cup shredded Cheddar cheese
- Six slices bacon diced
- Two slices of bread, cubed
- ⅓ red bell pepper, diced
- Two green onions, diced
- 3 tbsp. milk
- ½ tsp. minced garlic, or to taste
- salt and ground black pepper to taste

Directions:

1. Get the oven to a temperature of 350 degrees F. 175 degrees C.. A 9x13-inch pastry pan should be greased.
2. Before pouring into the prepared baking dish, mix the eggs, cheese, bacon, bread, red bell pepper, green onion, milk, garlic, salt, and black pepper together in a large bowl.
3. For 20–25 minutes in a preheated oven, or until eggs are firm.

16. French Toast

Ingredients:

- Four slices of bread
- Two eggs
- 1/4 cup milk
- 1 tbsp. sugar
- 1 tsp. vanilla extract
- 1/4 tsp. ground cinnamon
- Butter or oil for cooking
- Powdered sugar and maple syrup for serving

Instructions:

1. Whisk the eggs, milk, sugar, vanilla essence, and ground cinnamon in a shallow dish.
2. Make careful to cover both sides of each slice of bread when dipping it into the egg mixture.
3. When using a nonstick pan, a small amount of butter or oil should be added to the pan after it has been heated.
4. Once the butter has melted or the oil is hot, add the bread slices to the skillet and cook for two-three minutes on each side or until golden brown.
5. Continue with the leftover slices of bread.
6. Hot French toast should be served with powdered sugar and maple syrup.

17. Sheet Pan Breakfast Bake

Ingredients:

- 1 cup Greek yogurt
- One ¼ cup self-rising flour, plus more for kneading
- 1 tsp. carne asada seasoning
- cooking spray
- Five large eggs
- one cup shredded Colby cheese
- one cup frozen shredded hash brown potatoes, thawed
- two tbsp. salsa
- Four slices bacon
- green onions for garnish

Directions:

1. Preheat the oven to 175 degrees C (approximately 350 F). Prepare a baking sheet by spraying it with nonstick spray.
2. Combine the flour, Greek yogurt, and carne asada seasoning in a medium bowl. Stir until a shaggy dough develops. Transfer to a surface sprinkled with self-rising flour, and smooth out with a kneading motion for about 5 minutes. The mixture may need more flour if it is too sticky.
3. Five minutes of kneading should result in a smooth, uniform ball of dough.
4. The dough should be shaped to suit a sheet pan.
5. For 12 minutes, bake the dough in a prepared oven.
6. In the meantime, combine the hash browns, salsa, cheese, eggs, and cheese in a dish.

7. Bacon needs about 7 minutes in a big skillet over medium heat to brown evenly. Bacon should be transferred to a drip plate. Let the bacon cool before chopping it coarsely.
8. Over the dough, pour the egg concoction. Bacon is sprinkled on top.
9. If you want hard-boiled eggs, cook them for 25 minutes.
10. Green scallions should be diced and added after oven removal. Before serving, allow to chill slightly.

18. Spanish Potato Omelet

Ingredients:

- ½ cup olive oil
- ½ lb potatoes, thinly sliced
- salt and pepper to taste
- One large onion, thinly sliced
- Four large eggs
- Two medium tomatoes - peeled, seeded, and coarsely diced
- Two green onions, diced

Instructions:

1. A big pan with medium-high heat is used to heat the oil. Throw in the potatoes, and sprinkle a little salt and pepper on them. Stirring the potatoes occasionally, cook them for 10 to 14 minutes, until they are brown and crisp. Incorporate onions, cooking and stirring for 6-8 minutes until onions are soft and beginning to brown.
2. Beat the eggs in a bowl and season with salt and pepper. Stir softly as you pour the eggs into the skillet with the potatoes and onion. To achieve a golden brown bottom, cook the eggs for 4 to 5 minutes over medium heat.
3. Use a spoon to loosen the omelet. Flip the omelet out onto a wide plate that has been inverted over the pan. Return the uncooked half of the omelet to the pan. The eggs should be solid after four or five minutes

1. of cooking.

4. Tomatoes and green onions go well with the hot dish.

19. Overnight Oats

Ingredients:

- 1/2 cup rolled oats
- 1/2 cup milk
- 1/4 cup Greek yogurt
- 1 tbsp. Honey or maple syrup
- 1/2 tsp. vanilla extract
- Pinch of salt
- Toppings of your choice

Instructions:

1. Combine the oats, milk, yogurt, honey or maple syrup, vanilla extract, and salt in a jar or other receptacle.
2. Stir thoroughly to incorporate.
3. Overnight in the refrigerator, cover the container.
4. Top with your preferred garnishes and eat in the morning.

20. Breakfast Egg Muffins

Ingredients:

- Six eggs
- 1/4 cup milk
- 1/2 cup shredded cheese
- 1/2 cup diced vegetables
- Salt and pepper to taste

Instructions:

1. Cooking spray should grease a muffin tray as the oven is preheated to 350°F (180°C).
2. To make an egg dish, whisk together eggs, milk, salt, and pepper.
3. Add the cheese shavings and the diced veggies after that.
4. Prepare a muffin tin and fill each cup about two-thirds full with the mixture.
5. The egg cakes need 20–25 minutes in the oven, or until they are golden brown and set.
6. Wait a few minutes before removing from the muffin tin.

21. Quiche Lorraine

Ingredients:

- One pie crust
- Eight slices of bacon, diced
- One small onion, diced
- Four large eggs
- 1 cup heavy cream
- 1/2 tsp. salt
- 1/4 tsp. black pepper
- 1/8 tsp. ground nutmeg
- 1 1/2 cups shredded Swiss cheese

Instructions:

1. Set the oven's temperature to 375°F (190°C).
2. A 9-inch pie plate should be lined with the pie dough. Cut the edges, then put them away.
3. Cook the diced bacon to crispiness in a skillet over medium heat. Take out and drain on paper napkins after using the skillet.
4. The diced onion should be cooked until soft and translucent in the same pan. Get rid of the humidity.
5. Whisk the eggs, heavy cream, salt, pepper, and ground nutmeg in a medium dish.
6. Over the bottom of the pie crust, equally, distribute the cooked bacon and sautéed onion.
7. Over the bacon and onion, scatter the Swiss cheese.
8. Over the cheese, pour the egg concoction.
9. When the top of the quiche is golden, and the center is firm, bake it for thirty-five to forty minutes in a preheated oven.
10. Before slicing and serving the quiche, let it settle for a few minutes.

22. Veggie Breakfast Sandwich

Ingredients:

- 1 English muffin
- 1 egg, fried or scrambled
- 1/4 avocado, sliced
- 1/4 cup spinach leaves
- 1/4 cup sliced mushrooms
- One slice of cheddar cheese
- Salt and pepper to taste

Instructions:

1. The English muffin should be gently toasted.
2. You can cook or beat the egg to the desired doneness.
3. Cook the mushrooms in a little pan until they are soft.
4. On one side of the toasted English muffin, assemble the sandwich by adding the spinach leaves, sliced avocado, cooked egg, sautéed mushrooms, and cheddar cheese.
5. After adding a sprinkle of salt and pepper, the other muffin half should be positioned on top.

23. Huevos Rancheros

Ingredients:

- Two corn tortillas
- Two eggs, fried or scrambled
- 1/2 cup black beans, drained and rinsed
- 1/4 cup shredded cheddar cheese
- 1/4 cup salsa or hot sauce

Toppings:

- Diced tomatoes, sliced avocado, diced cilantro

Instructions:

1. Soften the tortillas by warming them in a dry pan over medium heat.
2. Add a fried or scrambled egg to each tortilla before placing it on a platter.
3. Add some grated cheddar cheese and black beans to the top of the eggs.
4. To flavor, drizzle on salsa or hot sauce.
5. You can put as many toppings as you like.

24. Yummy Veggie Omelet

Ingredients:

- 2 tbsp. butter, divided
- One small onion, diced
- One green bell pepper diced
- ¾ tsp. salt, divided
- Four large eggs
- 2 tbsp. Milk
- ⅛ tsp. freshly ground black pepper
- 2 oz. Shredded Swiss cheese

Instructions:

1. In a medium pan set over medium heat, melt 1 tbsp. Of butter. Cook and sauté onion and bell pepper in butter for 4–5 minutes, or until tender. Add 1/4 tsp. of salt to the bowl of vegetables before setting it away.
2. Combine the eggs, milk, and remaining 1/2 tsp in a different dish: salt and pepper.
3. Melt the last tbsp. Of butter in the pan over medium heat, then swirl it around to coat the bottom with butter. Pour egg mixture into bubbling butter and cook untouched for one minute or until the eggs' bottoms solidify. With a spatula, gently raise the omelet's edges, allowing any uncooked egg to drip onto the skillet. Keep cooking for another minute or two, or until the omelet seems set in the middle.
4. After topping the omelet with cheese, add the veggie mixture over half of it. Gently fold the omelet over the veggies using a spatula. To melt the cheddar to the desired consistency, cook for about a minute. The omelet has been prepared and served. To distribute, cut it in half.

25. Overnight Blueberry French Toast

Ingredients:

French Toast Casserole:

- 12 slices of day-old bread, cut into 1-inch cubes
- 2 (8 oz.) packages of cream cheese, cut into 1-inch cubes
- 1 cup fresh blueberries
- 12 eggs, beaten
- 2 cups milk
- 1 tsp. vanilla extract
- ⅓ cup maple syrup

Blueberry Sauce:

- 1 cup white sugar
- 1 cup water
- 2 tbsp. cornstarch
- 1 cup fresh blueberries
- 1 tbsp. butter

Instructions:

1. Cook a casserole: Grease a 9x13-inch baking dish very lightly. Place cream cheese pieces on top of half the bread cubes in the dish. The leftover bread cubes should be placed on the blueberries and cream cheese.
2. Combine the eggs, milk, vanilla extract, and syrup in a large bowl using a whisk. Pour the mixture over the bread cubes. Overnight, cover, and chill.
3. Thirty minutes before baking, take the casserole out of the oven. Get the oven to a temperature of 350 degrees F. 175 degrees C..
4. For 30 minutes, bake the casserole lidded in a preheated oven. Remove the cover, and bake for another 25 to 30 minutes until the center is firm and the top is lightly browned.

5. Prepare the blackberry sauce in the interim: In a medium saucepan, combine the sugar, water, and cornflour; boil and cook for three to four minutes while stirring continuously. Blueberries should start to explode after about 10 minutes of simmering, so stir them in after lowering the heat. Add butter and stir.
6. The warm syrup should be drizzled on top of the casserole pieces as they are served.

26. Oatmeal Soda Bread

Ingredients:

- 3 ½ cups all-purpose flour
- ½ cup quick cooking oats
- 1 tsp. salt
- 1 tsp. baking powder
- 1 tsp. baking soda
- 1 (8 oz.) container of low-fat sour cream
- ¾ cup of skim milk
- 2 tbsp. honey
- 1 tbsp. white sugar
- ¼ cup melted butter
- 2 tbsp. butter melted

Instructions:

1. Set oven to 375 degrees Fahrenheit. (190 degrees C).
2. Flour, 1/2 cup oats, salt, baking soda, and baking powder should be mixed together in a large bowl..
3. Combine the sour cream, milk, honey, and sugar in a separate dish. Stir briefly to incorporate, then add to the flour mixture.. Add softened butter or margarine and stir.
4. Put the dough on a baking tray that has been gently sprayed. Form into a circle about 8 inches in circumference and lightly mounded. Sprinkle the final spoonful of oats on the loaf after brushing it with melted butter or margarine. Slice the loaf's top into sections with a knife.
5. About 40 minutes, or until caramelized, in the oven. Slice only after the full cooling.

27. Crispy Fried Poached Eggs

Ingredients:

- Four large fresh eggs
- 2 tbsp. white vinegar
- 4 cups vegetable oil
- 1 ½ cups all-purpose flour
- Two large eggs, lightly beaten
- 2 tsp. salt
- 1 tsp. freshly ground black pepper
- 1 ½ cups panko bread crumbs
- 2 tbsp. diced pickled red onions
- 2 tbsp. diced green onions
- 1 tbsp. Red pepper flakes for garnish or to taste

Directions:

1. Put the cold water in a saucepan and set it over medium heat. After stirring in the vinegar, slow simmer for a few minutes. If you only use one egg at a time, it's easier to crack it into a dish or measuring cup.
2. To make a whirlpool, aggressively stir the water. Drop the egg into the water's middle as the vortex spins. Cooking the egg white until it becomes thick requires continued gentle stirring. Carefully extract the egg from the water using a slotted spoon, then transfer it to a plate covered in paper towels to drain.
3. Warm the oil in a skillet until it reaches 375 degrees Fahrenheit. degrees Celsius).
4. Establish a dredging station with three distinct containers in the interim. Add the flour to the first dish. In a different

dish, beat two eggs with salt and pepper. To the third dish, add breadcrumbs. To thoroughly coat the egg at each location, carefully dip the cooled egg into the flour, the egg mixture, and the breadcrumbs.

5. Carefully place the egg into the hot oil using a slotted spoon, and fry for 2 to 3 minutes or until golden brown, being cautious not to overcook. Pour onto a paper towel-lined plate to drain.
6. Add green scallions, pickled red onions, and red pepper flakes as garnish. Serve right away.

28. Breakfast Pork Cutlets

Ingredients:

Spice Mix:

- 1/4 tsp. whole fennel seeds
- 1/2 tsp. freshly ground black pepper
- 1/2 tsp. dried poultry seasoning
- 1/4 tsp. freshly ground nutmeg
- 1/4 tsp. garlic powder
- One pinch of cayenne pepper

Cutlet:

- 2 (6-8-oz.) boneless center-cut pork chops, trimmed
- 1 1/2 tsp. kosher salt
- 2 tsp. maple syrup
- 1/2 cup fine dry breadcrumbs
- 2 tbsp. olive oil
- 1 tbsp. butter

Directions:

1. In a mortar and pestle, crush the fennel seeds, then move them to a small bowl. Add the cayenne, black pepper, nutmeg, garlic powder, and chicken seasoning and stir.
2. Each pork chop should have several shallow vertical incisions made through the fat. Use a meat labor or another heavy flat object to lb each chop to a thickness of 1/4 inch by placing it between two sections of plastic wrap. Place on a platter.
3. Chops should be salted on both sides and dusted with the seasoning mixture. Chops should be coated with about half a tsp of maple sugar on each side.

4. Each chop should have breadcrumbs sprinkled on one side and tightly pressed in. Then, continue the process.
5. Butter and olive oil should be melted over medium heat in a nonstick skillet. Pork cutlets should be pan-fried for about 2 minutes per side, turning once, until the edges are browned and crisp and the flesh is no longer pink in the center. It should register 145 degrees F on an instant-read thermometer close to the center. (63 degrees C).

29. Sarah's Homemade Applesauce

Ingredients:

- Four apples - peeled, cored, and diced
- ¾ cup water
- ¼ cup white sugar
- ½ tsp. ground cinnamon

Instructions:

1. Put the apples, water, sugar, and cinnamon in a pan and cook over medium heat until the apples are soft, about 15 to 20 minutes.
2. Once the apple mixture has cooled, mash it with a fork or potato blender to the desired consistency.

30. Greek Yogurt Waffles

Ingredients:

- 2 cups all-purpose flour
- 2 tsp. baking powder
- 1/2 tsp. baking soda
- 1/2 tsp. salt
- 2 tbsp. granulated sugar
- 1 3/4 cups milk
- 1/2 cup plain Greek yogurt
- Two large eggs
- 1/4 cup unsalted butter, melted
- 1 tsp. vanilla extract

Instructions:

1. Warm up your pancake maker.
2. Combine the sugar, salt, baking powder, soda, and flour in a large bowl.
3. The milk, Greek yogurt, eggs, melted butter, and vanilla extract should be combined in a separate bowl.
4. After combining the wet and dry ingredients, the batter should be whisked until it is smooth.
5. Following the manufacturer's recommendations for the recommended quantity of batter and cooking time, scoop the batter onto the waffle iron.
6. Don't stop until every last bit of dough has been eaten.
7. You are serving the waffles hot with your choice of garnishes, such as fresh fruit, whipped cream, or maple syrup.

Lunch Recipes

31. Chicken Caesar Wrap

Ingredients:

- One large whole-wheat tortilla
- 2 cups diced romaine lettuce
- 1/2 cup cooked chicken breast, diced
- 1/4 cup grated Parmesan cheese
- 3 tbsp. Caesar dressing
- Salt and pepper to taste

Instructions:

1. Spread the Caesar dressing over the tortilla after laying it evenly.
2. Add the shredded Parmesan cheese, diced chicken breast, and romaine leaves.
3. Season the dish to taste with salt and pepper..
4. Serve the tortilla after rolling it firmly.

32. Delicious Egg Salad for Sandwiches

Ingredients:

- Eight eggs
- ½ cup mayonnaise
- ¼ cup diced green onion
- 1 tsp. prepared yellow mustard
- ¼ tsp. paprika
- salt and pepper to taste

Directions:

1. Put the eggs in a saucepan and then add the cold water.` Once the water has reached a rolling boil, turn off the heat. Allow the eggs to sit in the boiling water, covered, for 10 to 12 minutes. Peel, chop, and let cool after removing from boiling water.
2. Combine the diced eggs with the mustard, mayonnaise, and green onion in a dish. Prepare the seasoning by mixing in paprika, salt, and pepper. After stirring, serve with toast or biscuits.

33. Greek Salad

Ingredients:

- 2 cups diced romaine lettuce
- 1/2 cup cherry tomatoes, halved
- 1/2 cup cucumber, diced
- 1/4 cup red onion, thinly sliced
- 1/4 cup Kalamata olives
- 1/4 cup crumbled feta cheese
- 2 tbsp. olive oil
- 1 tbsp. red wine vinegar
- 1/2 tsp. dried oregano
- Salt and pepper to taste

Instructions:

1. Combine the lettuce, cherry tomatoes, cucumber, red onion, and Kalamata olives in a sizable dish.
2. To prepare the dressing, combine the olive oil, red wine vinegar, dried oregano, salt, and pepper in a small bowl.
3. After adding the dressing, toss the lettuce to combine.
4. The salad should be garnished with feta cheese crumbles before being served.

34. Veggie and Hummus Wrap

Ingredients:

- One large whole-wheat tortilla
- 1/4 cup hummus
- 1/2 cup diced raw vegetables
- 1/4 cup crumbled feta cheese
- Salt and pepper to taste

Instructions:

1. Spread the hummus over the tortilla after it has been laid evenly.
2. Add the feta cheese crumbles and diced raw veggies on top.
3. Season the dish to taste with salt and pepper..
4. Serve the tortilla after rolling it firmly.

35. Sloppy Joes

Ingredients:

- 1 lb lean ground beef
- ¼ cup diced onion
- ¼ cup diced green bell pepper
- ¾ cup ketchup, or to taste
- 1 tbsp. brown sugar, or to taste
- 1 tsp. yellow mustard, or to taste
- ½ tsp. garlic powder
- salt and ground black pepper to taste
- Six hamburger buns, split

Directions:

1. A giant skillet should be heated to medium. Lean ground beef should be cooked and stirred in a hot skillet for 3 to 4 minutes, or until some oil begins to render. Cook the meat and vegetables for three to five minutes or until the vegetables are soft and the beef is cooked.
2. Salt and pepper to taste; mix in ketchup, brown sugar, mustard, and garlic powder. Keep at a low boil for 20–30 minutes.
3. Distribute the beef mixture equally among the buns.

37. Veggie Wrap

Ingredients:

- One large whole-wheat tortilla
- 1/4 avocado, sliced
- 1/4 cup hummus
- 1/2 cup mixed greens
- 1/2 cup sliced cucumber
- 1/2 cup sliced bell pepper
- Salt and pepper to taste

Instructions:

1. Spread hummus over the center third of the tortilla wrap before laying it flat.
2. Sliced avocado should be placed on top of the hummus.
3. Place a bed of mixed greens, sliced cucumber, and sliced bell pepper atop the avocado.
4. Season the dish to taste with salt and pepper.
5. The tortilla's sides should be folded in and rolled up firmly.
6. To serve, split the wrap in two.

38. Best Cream of Broccoli Soup

Ingredients:

- 5 tbsp. butter, divided
- One onion, diced
- One stalk of celery, diced
- 3 cups chicken broth
- 8 cups broccoli florets
- 3 tbsp. all-purpose flour
- 2 cups milk
- ground black pepper to taste

Directions:

1. Assemble all the components.
2. In a small stockpot, melt 2 tsp of butter over medium heat. The onion and celery should be cooked until they are tender.
3. Cover and simmer the vegetables and broth for 10 minutes.
4. Fill the pitcher of the mixer no more than halfway with the soup as you pour it in. Hold the lid with a folded kitchen cloth when starting the blender. Use a few rapid pulses to get the soup moving in the blender before turning it on to puree. Pour into a clean saucepan after batch-pureeing until smooth. Alternatively, using an immersion mixer, you could puree the broth in the cooking pot.
5. Melt 3 tsp butter in a small saucepan over medium heat. of butter. Stir in the flour and milk. Add to broth and stir until thick and bubbly. Serve after adding pepper.

41. Avocado and Tomato Toast

Ingredients:

- Two slices of bread toasted
- One avocado, sliced
- 1/2 cup cherry tomatoes, halved
- 1/4 tsp. red pepper flakes
- Salt and pepper to taste

Instructions:

1. Sliced avocado and cherry tomatoes should be placed on each toast piece.
2. Spice it up with some salt, pepper, and crushed red pepper.

42. Pasta Salad

Ingredients:

- 1 lb tri-colored spiral pasta
- 1 (16 oz.) bottle of Italian-style salad dressing
- 6 tbsp. salad seasoning mix
- 2 cups cherry tomatoes, diced
- One green bell pepper, diced
- One red bell pepper, diced
- ½ yellow bell pepper, diced
- 1 (2.25 oz.) can of black olives, diced

Directions:

1. Assemble all the components.
2. A large pot of lightly salted water should be brought to a boil. Pasta should be prepared in water rapidly boiling for 10–12 minutes, stirring every few minutes until solid but tender: drain and cool-water flush.
3. Italian dressing and salad seasoning blend should be thoroughly combined in a bowl. Combine the pasta, tomatoes, bell peppers, and olives in a salad dish.
4. Sprinkle lettuce with dressing, then toss to combine.
5. Eight to twelve hours of refrigeration is recommended for salad.

43. Grilled Cheese Sandwich

Ingredients:

- Four slices of white bread
- 3 tbsp. butter, divided
- Two slices of Cheddar cheese

Directions:

1. A nonstick pan should be preheated to medium. Butter a piece of bread liberally on one side. Put one cheese slice and a buttered side of bread in a hot pan. A second piece of bread should be butter-side up and placed on the cheese.
2. Brown the bottom of the pizza, flip it, and cook until the cheese is melted. Repetition is required with the remaining two pieces of bread, butter, and cheese.

44. Ukrainian Red Borscht Soup

Ingredients:

- 1 (16 oz.) package of pork sausage
- Three medium beets peeled and shredded
- Three carrots, peeled and shredded
- 3 medium baking potatoes, peeled and cubed
- ½ medium head cabbage, cored and shredded
- 1 cup diced tomatoes, drained
- 1 tbsp. vegetable oil
- One medium onion, diced
- 1 (6 oz.) can of tomato paste
- Eight ¾ cups water, divided or as needed
- Three cloves garlic, minced
- 1 tsp. white sugar, or to taste
- salt and pepper to taste
- ½ cup sour cream for topping
- 1 tbsp. Diced fresh parsley for garnish

Directions:

1. In a skillet over medium-high heat, crumble pork. Cook while stirring until the redness is gone. Put the kettle out of its misery and walk away.
2. In a large saucepan, bring 8 cups of water to a boil, covering about half of the contents.
3. Put sausage in the saucepan, cover it, and bring it back to a boil. Beets should be added and cooked until they lose their color. Cook the potatoes and carrots until they are easily pierced with a fork, about 15 minutes.

4. Put the tomato dices and cabbage in the pan.
5. When the oil is hot, add the onion and cook it down until it's soft, about 5 minutes. The leftover 3/4 cup water and tomato paste should be thoroughly combined. Place in the saucepan.
6. Turn off the heat, cover the broth, and stir in the garlic. Wait for five minutes. Salt and pepper to taste, then stir in the sugar.
7. Into serving dishes, spoon. Add cilantro and sour cream as a garnish.

45. Homemade Corn Dogs

Ingredients:

- 1 cup yellow cornmeal
- 1 cup all-purpose flour
- ¼ cup white sugar
- Four tsp. baking powder
- ¼ tsp. salt
- ⅛ tsp. black pepper
- 1 cup milk
- One egg
- 1-quart vegetable oil for frying
- 2 (16 oz.) packages of beef frankfurters
- 16 wooden skewers

Directions:

1. The flour, cornmeal, sugar, baking powder, salt, and pepper should all be combined in a medium dish and whisked together. Use a blender to mix the milk and egg.

2. In a deep fryer or large saucepan, heat the oil to 375 degrees Fahrenheit. (190 degrees C). In the meantime, stab each frankfurter after drying it off with a paper towel. Frankfurters should be thoroughly covered in batter.

3. In the preheated oil, fry 2 or 3 corn dogs at once for about 3 minutes or until they are faintly browned. On paper napkins, drain.

46. Broccoli Cheese Soup

Ingredients:

- ½ cup butter
- One onion, diced
- 1 (16 oz.) package of frozen diced broccoli
- 4 (14.5 oz.) cans of chicken broth
- 1 (1 lb) loaf of processed cheese food, cubed
- 2 cups milk
- 1 tbsp. garlic powder
- ⅔ cup cornstarch
- 1 cup water

Directions:

1. In a stockpot set over medium heat, melt the butter. When the onion is added, cook it while periodically stirring until soft. Add vegetables and stir. For ten to fifteen minutes, or until broccoli is tender, add water and simmer.
2. Cut cheese into pieces and stir until melted on low heat. Add milk and garlic spice and stir.
3. In a small dish, whisk corn flour and water until thoroughly combined. Add to broth and heat through while frequently stirring until thick.

47. Caldo de Pollo

Ingredients:

- 5 lbs chicken leg quarters
- 2 gallons water
- 2 tbsp. minced garlic
- 2 tbsp. salt
- 1 tbsp. garlic powder
- 1 cube chicken bouillon
- Four large carrots peeled and cut into large chunks
- Four large potatoes peeled and cut into large chunks
- Four zucchini, cut into large chunks
- One chayote, cut into large chunks
- One large white onion, cut into large chunks
- ½ bunch of fresh cilantro diced

Directions:

1. Put the poultry legs in a sizable stockpot and cover it with water. Add salt, garlic powder, and diced garlic.
2. Over high heat, cover and come to a boil. Reduce the heat to a simmer and cook the chicken for an additional hour or two.
3. After dissolving the chicken bouillon cube, add the white onion, chayote, carrots, potatoes, and zucchini. Cover and cook on low heat for 45 minutes to an hour or until potatoes and carrots are tender.
4. Add broth with diced cilantro. After 5 minutes of simmering, serve.

48. Banh Mi

Ingredients:

- ½ cup rice vinegar
- ¼ cup white sugar
- ¼ cup water
- ¼ cup matchstick-cut carrots
- ¼ cup peeled and matchstick-cut daikon radish
- ¼ cup thinly sliced white onion
- one skinless, boneless chicken breast half
- one pinch of garlic salt, or to taste
- ground black pepper to taste one (12-inch)
- french baguette
- 4 tbsp. mayonnaise
- ¼ cup thinly sliced cucumber
- 1 tbsp. fresh cilantro leaves
- one small jalapeno pepper cut into 1/16-inch-thick matchsticks
- one wedge lime

Directions:

1. In a pot, mix water, sugar, and rice vinegar. Stirring for about a minute to help the sugar dissolve, bring to a simmer over medium heat. Laissez le mélange refroidir.
2. In a basin, combine the carrot, radish, and onion. Marinate for at least 30 minutes after adding the cooled vinegar mixture.
3. Put the baking sheet in the oven about 6 inches from the broiler while the vegetables marinate. Lightly grease a broiler

1. pan with slots.
4. Season the chicken breast with some salt, pepper, and diced garlic.
5. Turn the chicken over once during broiling and cook for 12 minutes.
6. Chicken should be put on a cutting block. Bite-sized portions should be cut.
7. Baguette should be cut in two lengthwise. Remove the bread's softcore, leaving a cavity for the fillings.
8. Under the broiler, lightly toast the bread for two to three minutes.
9. Vegetables should be drained of any extra vinegar combination after marinating.
10. Before assembling the sandwich, mayonnaise should be distributed on both halves of the baguette. On the bottom side of the bread, arrange the chicken. Add cilantro, jalapeno, cucumber, and drained pickled veggies as garnishes. Cover fillings with a lime wedge and the upper half of the baguette.
11. To serve, cut each sandwich into two 6-inch pieces.

49. Philly Steak Sandwich

Ingredients:

- ½ tsp. Salt
- ½ tsp. black pepper
- ½ tsp. paprika
- ½ teason chili powder
- ½ tsp. onion powder
- ½ tsp. garlic powder
- ½ tsp. dried thyme
- ½ tsp. dried marjoram
- ½ tsp. dried basil
- 1 lb beef sirloin, cut into thin 2-inch strips
- 3 tbsp. vegetable oil
- One onion, sliced
- 1 green bell pepper, julienned
- 3 oz. Swiss cheese, thinly sliced
- Four hoagie rolls split lengthwise

Directions:

1. Basil, thyme, marjoram, chili powder, paprika, onion powder, garlic powder, salt, and pepper
1. should be mixed in a small container.
2. Put all of the beef into a large bowl. Mix well to coat everything equally with the seasoning blend.
3. In a skillet, heat half of the oil over low to medium heat. When the beef is done, throw it in the pan and keep cooking. Remove to a serving plate.
4. The skillet is heating with the leftover oil. Add the onion and green pepper, then cook until they are soft.
5. Set the grill setting on the oven.
6. On the bottoms of 4 rolls, divide the cooked meat. Add onion and green pepper to the layer before adding cheddar slices. On a cookie tray, place.
7. Until the cheese is softened, broil in the preheated oven.
8. Serve the rolls with their top tips.

50. Pasta Salad with Homemade Dressing

Ingredients:

- 1 (8 oz.) package of uncooked tri-color rotini pasta
- 6 oz. pepperoni sausage, diced
- 6 oz. provolone cheese, cubed
- One medium red onion, very thinly sliced and cut into 1-inch pieces
- 1 small cucumber, thinly sliced
- ¾ cup diced green bell pepper
- ¾ cup diced red bell pepper
- 1 (6 oz.) can of pitted black olives, drained
- ¼ cup minced fresh parsley
- ¼ cup grated Parmesan cheese

Dressing:

- ½ cup olive oil
- ¼ cup red wine vinegar
- Two cloves garlic, minced
- 1 tsp. dried basil
- 1 tsp. dried oregano
- ½ tsp. ground mustard seed
- ¼ tsp. Salt
- ⅛ tsp. Ground black pepper

Directions:

1. Assemble all the components.
2. To begin, bring a large pot of lightly salted water to a boil. Cook the rotini for 8 to 10 minutes in the simmering sauce, or until it is al dente. Drain once more after rinsing with cool water.

3. Place cooked, drained spaghetti in a big bowl. Add the following ingredients: pepperoni, provolone cheese, red onion, cucumber, bell peppers, olives, cilantro, and Parmesan cheese.
4. In a container with a lid, combine the dressing ingredients: olive oil, vinegar, garlic, basil, oregano, ground mustard, salt, and pepper. Shake vigorously while tightening the lid of the container.
5. Dress the macaroni salad and stir to combine; it’s done. Cover and refrigerate for up to 8 hours before serving.

51. Three Bean Salad

Ingredients:

- 1 (15 oz.) can think of green beans
- 1 lb wax beans
- one (15 oz.) can of kidney beans, drained and rinsed
- 1 onion, sliced into thin rings
- ¾ cup white sugar, or to taste
- ⅔ cup distilled white vinegar
- ⅓ cup vegetable oil
- ½ tsp. salt
- ½ tsp. ground black pepper
- ½ tsp. celery seed

Directions:

1. Assemble all the components.
2. Green beans, kidney beans, wax beans, onion, sugar, vinegar, vegetable oil, salt, and celery seed should all be combined. Refrigerate for a minimum of 12 hours.

52. Easy French Dip Sandwiches

Ingredients:

- Four hoagie rolls split lengthwise
- 1 (10.5 oz.) can of beef consommé
- 1 cup water
- 1 lb thinly sliced deli roast beef
- 8 slices provolone cheese

Directions:

1. Get the oven to a temperature of 350 degrees F. 175 degrees C..
2. Hoagie should be opened and spread out on a baking sheet.
3. In a medium saucepan, bring the water and beef consommé to a boil over medium heat. This will yield a flavorful beef broth.
4. Warm the roast meat in the broth for three minutes.
5. Spread the meat mixture on the hoagie rolls, then top with two slices of provolone cheese.
6. To melt the cheese on a sandwich, put it in a preheated oven for about five minutes.
7. Small bowls of hot broth go great with sandwiches.

53. Zesty Quinoa Salad

Ingredients:

- 2 cups water
- 1 cup quinoa
- ¼ cup extra-virgin olive oil
- Two limes, juiced
- 2 tsp. ground cumin
- 1 tsp. salt
- ½ tsp. red pepper flakes, or more to taste
- 1 ½ cups halved cherry tomatoes
- one (15 oz.) can of black beans, drained and rinsed
- Five green onions, finely diced
- ¼ cup diced fresh cilantro
- salt and ground black pepper to taste

Directions:

1. Put the rice and water in a saucepan and come to a boil. Simmer, covered, for 10 to 15 minutes, or until water is consumed and the quinoa is soft. Put aside to chill down.
2. While waiting, prepare a small serving of the marinade by combining olive oil, lime juice, cumin, salt, and red pepper flakes.
3. Mix the quinoa, tomatoes, black beans, and green onions in a sizable dish. Toss the quinoa combination with the dressing to coat. Parsley, salt, and black pepper to taste. Serve right away, or let the food cool in the fridge.

54. Garlic Bread Spread

Ingredients:

- ½ cup softened butter
- ¼ cup grated Parmesan cheese
- Two cloves garlic, minced
- ¼ tsp. dried marjoram
- ¼ tsp. dried basil
- ¼ tsp. fines herbs
- ¼ tsp. dried oregano
- ¼ tsp. dried parsley or to taste
- ground black pepper to taste
- One loaf of unsliced Italian bread

Directions:

1. Assemble the components, and then heat the oven to 350°F. (175 degrees C).
2. Butter, Parmesan cheese, garlic, thyme, basil, oregano, parsley, fine herbs, and pepper should all be combined.
3. Split the loaf of Italian bread down the middle lengthwise and slather each side with the garlic butter mixture. Transfer to a baking sheet.
4. Put the baking dish on the oven's highest rack and bake for 10 to 15 minutes, or until the butter mixture melts and bubbles. Broil the bread for one to two more minutes, depending on the desired level of golden brown, using the oven's broiler.

55. Simple Pasta Salad

Ingredients:

- 1 (16 oz.) package of uncooked rotini pasta
- 1 (16 oz.) bottle of Italian salad dressing
- Two cucumbers diced
- Six tomatoes, diced
- One bunch of green onions, diced
- Four oz. grated Parmesan cheese
- 1 tbsp. Italian seasoning

Directions:

1. Assemble all the components.
2. To begin, bring a large pot of lightly salted water to a boil.. Pasta should be added to the saucepan and cooked for 8 to 12 minutes or until al dente.
3. Combine cooked pasta, Italian dressing, cucumbers, tomatoes, and green onions in a sizable dish. Mix the Parmesan and Italian seasoning in a small bowl. Mix the ingredients gently and add them to the salad.
4. Keep chilled for at least 30 minutes before serving, covered.

56. Egg salad

Ingredients:

- Six hard-boiled eggs, peeled and diced
- 1/4 cup mayonnaise
- 1 tsp. Dijon mustard
- 1/4 tsp. garlic powder
- Salt and pepper, to taste
- Diced chives or parsley

Instructions:

1. The diced hard-boiled eggs, mayonnaise, Dijon mustard, and garlic powder should all be thoroughly combined in a dish.
2. Season the dish to taste with salt and pepper..
3. Add some finely diced chives or parsley for flavor and color if preferred.
4. The egg salad can be served as a sandwich, on a bed of vegetables, or with crackers.

57. Pita pockets with hummus and veggies

Ingredients:

- Four whole-wheat pita pockets
- 1 cup hummus
- 1/2 cup diced cucumber
- 1/2 cup diced tomato
- 1/4 cup sliced red onion
- 1/4 cup sliced Kalamata olives
- 1/4 cup crumbled feta cheese
- Fresh parsley leaves, for garnish

Instructions:

1. To make eight pockets, divide the bread pockets in half.
2. Each compartment should have 2 tbsp of hummus inside.
3. Put the sliced cucumber, tomato, red onion, and Kalamata olives inside the pockets.
4. Over the vegetables, sprinkle feta cheese crumbles.
5. If preferred, garnish with new parsley leaves.
6. Pita pockets can be served as a light meal or snack.

58. Black bean and sweet potato tacos

Ingredients:

- 2 large sweet potatoes, peeled and diced
- 2 tbsp. olive oil
- 1 tsp. chili powder
- 1/2 tsp. ground cumin
- 1/4 tsp. paprika
- Salt and pepper, to taste
- one can (15 oz.) of black beans, drained and rinsed
- 1/2 cup diced red onion
- 1/2 cup diced fresh cilantro
- 8 small flour or corn tortillas

Toppings:

- Sliced avocado, crumbled queso fresco, lime wedges, hot sauce

Instructions:

1. Set the oven's temperature to 400°F (200°C).
2. Sweet potatoes should be diced and well-coated in a dish with olive oil, chili powder, cumin, paprika, salt, and pepper.
3. On a baking pan, spread the sweet potatoes out and roast for 20 to 25 minutes, or until fork-tender and lightly browned.
4. Combine the black beans, red onion, and cilantro in a separate dish.
5. The tortillas can be warmed on a grill or in the oven.

6. Spoon some sweet potato and black bean mixture onto each tortilla to assemble the tacos.
7. Add extras like diced avocado, queso fresco crumbles, lime wedges, or hot sauce.
8. Tacos are made by folding the tortillas in half, then served right away.

Dinner Recipes

59. Chicken stir-fry

Ingredients:

- one lb boneless, skinless chicken breasts cut into thin strips
- 2 tbsp. vegetable oil
- One red bell pepper, seeded and thinly sliced
- One yellow bell pepper, seeded and thinly sliced
- One onion, thinly sliced
- 1 tbsp. minced garlic
- 1 tbsp. minced ginger
- 2 tbsp. soy sauce
- 2 tbsp. oyster sauce
- Salt and pepper, to taste
- Cooked rice for serving

Instructions:

1. Heat the veggie oil over high heat
2. in a big wok or skillet.
3. The chicken needs to be stir-fried for about four minutes or until it is colored and cooked through. Put away and put the skillet away.
4. The same pan should be used to stir-fry the bell peppers, onion, garlic, and ginger for 2 to 3 minutes or until the veggies are crisp-tender.
5. Stir in soy and oyster sauce to coat the veggies in the pan.
6. To thoroughly reheat the chicken, put it back in the pan and stir-fry for one more minute.
7. The dish needs salt and pepper to bring out the flavor.
8. Stir-fry should be served with prepared rice. Enjoy!

60. Corned Beef Roast

Ingredients:

- 1 (5 1/2 lb) corned beef brisket with spice packet
- Seven small potatoes, peeled and diced
- Four carrots, peeled and diced
- One medium onion, diced
- Three cloves garlic, diced

Directions:

1. Set the oven to 300 degrees Fahrenheit. (150 degrees C).
2. In the center of a roasting skillet, place the corned beef brisket. Potatoes and carrots should be placed around the edges, and beef should be topped with onion and garlic. Cover the potatoes with water almost to the top and sprinkle the meat with the seasoning packet's contents. Use a lid or thick aluminum sheet to cover.
3. Corned beef should be roasted in the preheated oven for 5 to 6 hours or until it can easily be broken apart with a fork.

61. Lasagna Flatbread

Ingredients:

- 1 (15 oz.) container of ricotta cheese
- 1 (8 oz.) package of shredded mozzarella cheese divided
- 1 (3 oz.) package of Parmesan cheese
- One egg
- 2 tsp. Italian seasoning
- 1 lb sausage
- ½ (26 oz.) jar marinara sauce
- Six flatbreads

Directions:

1. Turn the oven temperature up to 375 degrees F. degrees Celsius).
2. Mix the ricotta cheese, half the mozzarella cheese, the Parmesan cheese, the egg, and the Italian seasoning in a dish.
3. Sausage should be cooked in a pan over medium heat for 5 to 10 minutes or until no longer pink. Drain. Add tomato sauce and stir.
4. Evenly distribute 1/6 of the cheese combination on each flatbread, then top with the sausage mixture. Top with the remaining mozzarella cheese.
5. Heat in an oven until bubbling and the cheese is melted, about 10 to 15 minutes.

62. Mississippi Chicken

Ingredients:

- 2 lbs skinless, boneless chicken breasts
- The dry ranch dressing mix of your choice, such as Hidden Valley Ranch®, 1 ounce
- 1 (16 oz.) jar of sliced pepperoncini peppers, drained
- 4 tbsp. Unsalted butter, sliced

Directions:

1. Get the oven to a temperature of 350 degrees F. 175 degrees C..
2. Season the chicken with ranch seasoning blend and lay it in the bottom of a large Dutch oven. Over the poultry, add butter, pepperoncini peppers, and 1/2 cup of reserved pepper juice. The poultry should be fork tender for about 1 hour and 30 minutes, covered in a preheated oven. The internal temperature, as measured by an instant-read thermometer, should be 165 degrees Fahrenheit. (74 degrees C).
3. Wait for five minutes. Use two forks to shred the poultry.

63. Juicy Roasted Chicken

Ingredients:

- 1 (3 lb) whole chicken, giblets removed
- salt and black pepper to taste
- 1 tbsp. onion powder, or to taste
- ½ cup butter or margarine
- One stalk of celery, leaves removed

Directions:

1. Get the oven to a temperature of 350 degrees F. 175 degrees C..
2. Season the chicken with salt, pepper, and onion powder on both the inside and outside of a roasting pan, and then set it in the oven. Put three tbsp. of the leftover butter in the cavity of the chicken and place dollops of it on the outside. Place three or four sections of celery cut into it the cavity of the chicken.
3. In a preheated oven, bake the chicken uncovered for about 1 hour and 15 minutes, or until the juices flow clear and the meat is no longer pink at the bone. An instant-read thermometer inserted into the thickest part of the thigh, close to the bone, should show a temperature of 165 degrees Fahrenheit. (74 degrees C).
4. Take out of the oven, then slather with drippings. Before serving, let the food settle for about 30 minutes under a foil cover.

64. Chicken Pot Pie

Ingredients:

- 1 lb skinless, boneless chicken breast halves - cubed
- 1 cup sliced carrots
- 1 cup frozen green peas
- ½ cup sliced celery
- ⅓ cup butter
- ⅓ cup diced onion
- ⅓ cup all-purpose flour
- ½ tsp. salt
- ¼ tsp. black pepper
- ¼ tsp. celery seed
- One ¾ cups chicken broth
- ⅔ cup milk
- 2 (9-inch) unbaked pie crusts

Directions:

1. Assemble all the components.
2. Turn the oven temperature up to 425 degrees. heat to 220 degrees.
3. Put the chicken, vegetables, and seasonings into a pot. Just add water, and bring to a boil. When the water reaches a boil, turn off the heat and pour it out after 15 minutes.
4. In a separate pan, melt the butter over medium heat while the chicken is cooking. For 5–7 minutes, or until soft and translucent, simmer the onion in the sauce. Add the flour, celery powder, and seasonings.
5. Add milk and poultry broth gradually. Reduce heat to medium-low, then boil for 5 to 10 minutes until thick. Heat has been removed; put aside.
6. Put the chicken and veggies in the pie crust's bottom layer. Overtop, pour the hot liquid concoction. Remove any extra dough before covering it with the top crust and sealing the

sides. To let steam out, make several tiny slits in the upper crust.

7. Put in the oven and bake for 30–35 minutes, or until the pastry is golden and the filling is bubbling. Before serving, let cool for ten minutes.

65. Spaghetti Carbonara

Ingredients:

- 1 lb spaghetti
- 1/2 lb bacon, diced
- 1 cup grated Parmesan cheese
- Four large egg yolks
- Two cloves garlic, minced
- 1/2 tsp. black pepper
- Salt, to taste

Instructions:

1. Follow the directions on the spaghetti box for cooking. Drain, then set apart.
2. Cook the pork to crispiness in a sizable skillet over medium-high heat. Put away the skillet, please.
3. The Parmesan cheese, egg yolks, garlic, black pepper, and salt should all be combined in a dish.
4. Pasta should be combined with the bacon in a skillet after cooking.
5. After turning off the heat, pour the egg mixture into the skillet and rapidly stir in the spaghetti. The spaghetti's heat will cook the egg combination, resulting in a creamy sauce.
6. Serve right away with more Parmesan cheese and black pepper on top.

66. Grilled Lemon Chicken with Asparagus

Ingredients:

- Four boneless, skinless chicken breasts
- 1/4 cup olive oil
- 3 tbsp. lemon juice
- Two cloves garlic, minced
- 1/2 tsp. salt
- 1/4 tsp. black pepper
- 1 lb asparagus spears, trimmed
- 1 tbsp. Grated Parmesan cheese

Instructions:

1. Heat the grill to medium-high.
2. Ideally, a dish would include the following ingredients: olive oil, lemon juice, garlic, salt, black pepper.
3. Toss the chicken breasts in the marinade after adding them to the dish. Wait 10 minutes, at the very least.
4. Cook the chicken on a grill for 6–8 minutes per side, or until an instant-read thermometer registers 165 degrees.
5. Arrange the asparagus on the grill and cook for 2–3 minutes per side, or until fork- tender and faintly charred, while the chicken cooks.
6. Place the grilled chicken, asparagus, and Parmesan cheese on a serving plate.

67. Vegetarian Chili

Ingredients:

- 1 tbsp. olive oil
- One onion, diced
- Three cloves garlic, minced
- One red bell pepper, diced
- One green bell pepper, diced
- Two jalapeño peppers, seeded and minced
- 1 tbsp. chili powder
- 1 tbsp. ground cumin
- 1 tsp. smoked paprika
- One can (28 oz.) of diced tomatoes, undrained
- Two cans (15 oz. each) of kidney beans, rinsed and drained
- One can (15 oz.) of black beans, rinsed and drained
- 1 cup vegetable broth
- Salt and black pepper, to taste
- Shredded cheddar cheese and diced
- fresh cilantro for garnish

Instructions:

1. The olive oil should be heated in a big pot or Dutch oven over medium heat.
2. Add bell peppers, jalapenos, onion, garlic, and sauté until soft.
3. After adding them, stir in the cumin, smoky paprika, and chili powder.
4. Bring to a simmer after adding the diced tomatoes, kidney beans, black beans, and veggie broth.

5. Season the food with salt and pepper to taste.
6. Stirring periodically, reduce the heat to low, cover, and simmer the chili for 30 to 40 minutes.
7. Top hot dishes with diced fresh cilantro and cheddar cheese shavings if preferred.

68. Pan-Seared Salmon with Broccoli and Quinoa

Ingredients:

- 4 (6-oz.) skin-on salmon fillets
- 2 tbsp. olive oil
- Salt and black pepper, to taste
- One head of broccoli diced into florets
- 1 cup quinoa
- 2 cups vegetable broth
- 1 tbsp. diced fresh parsley
- Lemon wedges for serving

Instructions:

1. One spoonful of olive oil is heated to medium-high heat in a big skillet.
2. Salt and pepper the salmon fillets before placing them skin-side down in the pan.
3. Cook the salmon for at least four and a half minutes on each side to ensure it is thoroughly cooked.
4. While the fish is in the oven, steam the broccoli until it is just tender.
5. In a medium saucepan, bring the vegetable broth and quinoa to a boil. Once the liquid has been consumed and the quinoa is tender, turn the heat down to low, cover the pot, and let it simmer for 15 to 20 minutes.
6. With a spatula, fluff the quinoa, then stir in the parsley.
7. With steamed broccoli on the side, plate the pan-seared salmon over rice. Salmon should be topped with lemon slices for enjoyment.

69. Vegetable Stir Fry with Tofu

Ingredients:

- One block (14-16 oz.) of firm tofu, drained and cubed
- 2 tbsp. cornstarch
- Salt and black pepper, to taste
- 1/4 cup vegetable oil
- One onion, diced
- Two cloves garlic, minced
- One red bell pepper, sliced
- One green bell pepper, sliced
- 1 cup sliced mushrooms
- 1 cup diced broccoli
- 1 cup snow peas
- 1/4 cup soy sauce
- 1 tbsp. honey
- 1 tbsp. rice vinegar
- 1 tbsp. grated ginger
- 2 tbsp. Diced fresh cilantro

Instructions:

1. Turn the oven on to 375°F.
2. Tofu cubes should be equally coated after mixing with cornstarch, salt, and black pepper in a bowl.
3. In a large pan or wok, heat the vegetable oil until very hot.
4. For 5–7 minutes, or until the tofu is golden, stir-fry the pieces. Remove from heat and set aside.
5. Add the onion, garlic, bell peppers, mushrooms, broccoli, and snow peas to the same pan. Vegetables should be stir-fried for 5-7 minutes or until crisp-tender.
6. In a tiny bowl, combine the soy sauce, honey, rice vinegar, and minced ginger.

7. When the tofu and vegetables are done, pour the sauce over them in the skillet. Mix everything together, then heat for a minute or two.
8. Serve heatedly with fresh cilantro that has been diced.

70. Garlic Butter Shrimp with Zucchini Noodles

Ingredients:

- 1 lb large shrimp, peeled and deveined
- Salt and black pepper, to taste
- 4 tbsp. unsalted butter
- Four cloves garlic, minced
- 1/4 tsp. red pepper flakes
- 4 medium zucchinis, spiralized
- 2 tbsp. diced fresh parsley leaves
- 1 lemon, cut into wedges

Instructions:

1. Put some salt and black pepper on the shrimp.
2. Butter should be melted in a large skillet over low to medium heat.
3. To release their aroma, red pepper flakes and garlic should be sautéed for 1-2 minutes.
4. After 3–4 minutes, when the shrimp are pink and opaque all the way through, add them to the pan.
5. Take the shrimp out of the pan and set them aside.
6. In the same skillet, add the spiralized zucchini and cook for 2–3 minutes or until they are soft and barely browned.
7. Add the prawns back to the skillet and stir in the zucchini.
8. To flavor, add salt and black pepper to the dish.
9. Garnish with parsley and lemon slices before serving.

71. One Pot Chicken Alfredo

Ingredients:

- One lb boneless, skinless chicken breasts cut into bite-sized pieces
- Salt and black pepper, to taste
- 2 tbsp. olive oil
- Four cloves garlic, minced
- 4 cups chicken broth
- 1 lb fettuccine pasta
- 1 cup heavy cream
- 1 cup grated Parmesan cheese
- 2 cups baby spinach

Instructions:

1. Before serving, season the chicken with salt and pepper..
2. Olive oil should be heated in a large saucepan or Dutch oven over medium heat.
3. A total of 5-7 minutes should pass after adding the poultry for it to brown on all sides.
4. When aromatic, add the garlic and cook for 1-2 minutes.
5. Bring the fettuccine noodles, chicken broth, and other ingredients to a boil in a pot.
6. Turn the heat down to low, cover the pan, and let the spaghetti simmer for 12 to 15 minutes.
7. After adding the heavy cream and Parmesan cheese, let the sauce simmer for a couple of minutes until it thickens and becomes velvety.
8. Baby greens should be added and stirred until it wilts.
9. If preferred, top with more Parmesan cheese when serving.

72. Turkey and Spinach Stuffed Shells

Ingredients:

- 12 jumbo pasta shells
- 1 tbsp. olive oil
- 1/2 onion, diced
- Two cloves garlic, minced
- 1 lb ground turkey
- Salt and black pepper, to taste
- 1 tsp. Italian seasoning
- one cup frozen diced spinach, thawed and drained
- one cup of ricotta cheese
- One egg
- 1/4 cup grated Parmesan cheese
- 1 1/2 cups marinara sauce
- 1 cup shredded mozzarella cheese

Instructions:

1. The pasta shells should be prepared per the directions on the box, drained, and stored.
2. Preheat the oven to 165 degrees Celsius.
3. In a large skillet, melt the olive oil over low to medium heat.
4. To soften the onion and garlic, sauté them for 5–7 minutes.
5. While cooking, break up the ground turkey into tiny pieces with a spatula as it browns and cooks through. Mix in the ground turkey, seasonings, salt, and pepper.
6. After adding the greens, stir them in, and turn off the heat.

7. Combine the ricotta cheese, egg, and Parmesan cheese in a different dish.
8. Cover the bottom of a 9-by-13-inch baking dish with a thin layer of marinara sauce.
9. Place the filled pasta shells in the baking dish after stuffing each cooked pasta shell with a spoonful of the meat mixture.
10. Top the stuffed shells with the leftover marinara sauce.
11. Grate some mozzarella cheese and sprinkle it on top of the sauce.
12. Bake the casserole for 25 minutes while it is covered with aluminum foil.
13. Bake until the cheese is melted and bubbling, about 10 to 15 minutes after removing the paper.
14. Before serving, allow the filled shells to cool for five to ten minutes.

73. Beef and Broccoli Stir Fry

Ingredients:

- 1 lb beef sirloin, sliced thinly against the grain
- Salt and black pepper, to taste
- 2 tbsp. vegetable oil
- Two cloves garlic, minced
- 1 tsp. fresh ginger, grated
- 1/4 cup soy sauce
- 2 tbsp. brown sugar
- 2 tbsp. cornstarch
- 1/2 cup beef broth
- 2 cups broccoli florets
- One red bell pepper, sliced
- Cooked rice for serving

Instructions:

1. Black pepper and salt are used to season the meat.
2. In a large skillet or wok, heat the vegetable oil over high heat.
3. Brown the meat on all sides by stir-frying it for two to three minutes. Take the beef out of the skillet and set it aside.
4. Garlic and ginger should be stir-fried for 1-2 minutes, or until fragrant.
5. Soy sauce, brown sugar, cornstarch, and beef broth should be thoroughly combined in a small dish.
6. For 3–4 minutes, or until broccoli and red bell pepper are crisp-tender, stir-fry the vegetables in the pan.
7. Add the soy sauce mixture to the pan with the meat.
8. To ensure the meat is cooked through and the sauce has thickened, cook it for another 2–3 minutes.
9. Serve over hot, cooked rice.

74. Baked Parmesan Crusted Chicken with Roasted Vegetables

Ingredients:

- Four boneless, skinless chicken breasts
- Salt and black pepper, to taste
- 1/2 cup all-purpose flour
- 1 tsp. garlic powder
- 1 tsp. onion powder
- Two eggs, beaten
- 1 cup breadcrumbs
- 1/2 cup grated Parmesan cheese
- 2 tbsp. olive oil
- 4 cups mixed vegetables (such as broccoli, carrots, and bell peppers), diced into bite- sized pieces

Instructions:

1. Set the oven to 400°F.
2. Before serving, season the chicken with salt and pepper..
3. Mix the flour, onion powder, and garlic powder in a shallow bowl.
4. Separately, whisk the egg yolks.
5. In a third bowl, mix together the bread crumbs and Parmesan.
6. As you coat each chicken breast in flour, shake off the excess.
7. Before covering it with the breadcrumb mixture, dip the poultry into the beaten eggs.

8. Prepare a baking sheet lined with parchment paper and lay out the chicken.
9. Drizzle olive oil over the chicken.
10. In a separate bowl, toss the diced vegetables with the olive oil, salt, and pepper.
11. On the baking sheet, distribute the vegetables all around the poultry.
12. Cook for 20–25 minutes, or until chicken is no longer pink and vegetables are tender.

75. Creamy Pesto Pasta with Chicken and Sun-Dried Tomatoes

Ingredients:

- 8 oz. pasta (linguine or fettuccine)
- Two boneless, skinless chicken breasts
- Salt and pepper, to taste
- 2 tbsp. olive oil
- 1/4 cup sun-dried tomatoes, diced
- 1/4 cup pesto sauce
- 1/2 cup heavy cream
- 1/2 cup grated Parmesan cheese
- Fresh basil, diced

Instructions:

1. Follow the directions on the pasta box for cooking. Drain, then set apart.
2. Sprinkle some salt and pepper on the poultry.
3. In a large pan over medium heat, warm the olive oil.
4. Turn the chicken over after 6–8 minutes, or until cooked through..
5. After removing the poultry from the pan, rest for five minutes. Make pieces out of it.
6. In the same skillet, add the sun-dried tomatoes and cook for one to two minutes.
7. Mix in the pesto sauce and the heavy cream.
8. Toss the cooked linguine and chicken slices in the sauce in the pan.
9. Add fresh basil as a garnish and top with Parmesan cheese if preferred.
10. Serve warm.

76. Fish Tacos with Mango Salsa

Ingredients:

- 1 lb white fish
- Salt and black pepper, to taste
- 1 tbsp. olive oil
- 8-10 small corn tortillas
- 1 cup shredded cabbage
- 1/4 cup fresh cilantro, diced
- One avocado, sliced
- Lime wedges for serving

For the Mango Salsa:

- One ripe mango, diced
- 1/2 red onion, diced
- 1/2 red bell pepper, diced
- 1/4 cup fresh cilantro, diced
- One jalapeño pepper, seeded and finely diced
- 1 tbsp. lime juice

Instructions:

1. Black pepper and salt are used to season the seafood.
2. In a large skillet, melt the butter over medium heat and add the olive oil.
3. When cooking fish, remove it from the pan and cut it into small pieces.
4. The tortillas can be warmed on a skillet or in the oven.
5. Mangos that have been diced, red onions, red bell peppers, cilantro, jalapenos, and lime juice should all be combined in a bowl to create the mango salsa.

6. Before assembling the tacos, spread some diced cabbage on each tortilla.
7. Add the prepared fish, mango salsa, and avocado slices.
8. Accompany with lime wedges and top with chopped cilantro.

77. Sausage and Vegetable Skillet

Ingredients:

- 1 lb Italian sausage, sliced
- 1 tbsp. olive oil
- One red bell pepper, sliced
- One yellow bell pepper, sliced
- One onion, sliced
- One zucchini, sliced
- Salt and black pepper, to taste
- 1 tbsp. Italian seasoning
- 1/2 cup chicken broth
- 1/2 cup grated Parmesan cheese
- Fresh parsley, diced

Instructions:

1. The olive oil must be heated over medium heat in a big skillet.
2. Sauté the pork slices in the pan for 6 to 8 minutes or until browned.
3. Sausage should be taken out of the pan and put away.
4. Sliced peppers, onions, and zucchini should all be added to the skillet.
5. Italian seasoning, black pepper, and salt are used to season the veggies.
6. Vegetables should be cooked for 8–10 minutes or until soft.
7. Add the chicken broth and add the meat back to the pan.
8. To slightly decrease the broth, cook for another two to three minutes.
9. If preferred, garnish with fresh parsley and a sprinkle of Parmesan cheese.
10. Serve warm.

78. Lemon Butter Chicken with Asparagus

Ingredients:

- Four boneless, skinless chicken breasts
- Salt and black pepper, to taste
- 2 tbsp. olive oil
- 1 tbsp. butter
- 1/4 cup chicken broth
- 1/4 cup lemon juice
- Two cloves garlic, minced
- 1 lb asparagus, trimmed and cut into 2-inch pieces
- Lemon wedges for serving

Instructions:

1. Before serving, season the chicken with salt and pepper..
2. In a large pan over medium heat, olive oil should be heated.
3. Turn the chicken over after 6–8 minutes, or until cooked through..
4. After removing the poultry from the pan, rest for five minutes.
5. Butter should be melted in the same skillet over medium heat.
6. Lemon juice, minced garlic, and chicken stock should all be added to the pan.
7. Cooking for just two or three minutes will result in a negligible volume loss.
8. Once you've added the asparagus to the pan with the sauce, toss it to coat.

9. The asparagus should be cooked for 4-5 minutes or until tender.
10. Lemon wedges should be served with poultry and asparagus.

79. Slow Cooker Beef and Vegetable Soup

Ingredients:

- 1 lb beef stew meat
- One onion, diced
- Three garlic cloves minced
- 4 cups beef broth
- One can dice tomatoes (14.5 oz)
- Three large carrots, sliced
- Three celery stalks, sliced
- 2 cups potatoes, diced
- 1 tsp. dried thyme
- One bay leaf
- Salt and black pepper, to taste
- 1 cup frozen peas

Instructions:

1. Combine the beef stew meat, carrots, celery, potatoes, diced tomatoes, onion, garlic, beef stock, thyme, and bay leaf in a slow cooker.
2. Mix everything together.
3. I put it on low for eight hours, or high for four.
4. Add the frozen peas during the last 30 minutes of simmering.
5. Before serving, throw away the bay leaf.
6. Serve warm.

80. Sheet Pan Sausage and Veggie Dinner

Ingredients:

- 4 Italian sausages
- One red bell pepper, sliced
- One yellow bell pepper, sliced
- One onion, sliced
- One zucchini, sliced
- 1 tbsp. olive oil
- Salt and black pepper, to taste
- 1 tsp. dried oregano
- 1 tsp. garlic powder
- 1/2 tsp. paprika
- Fresh parsley, diced

Instructions:

1. Set the oven's temperature to 400°F (200°C).
2. Arrange the Italian sausages, bell peppers, onion, and zucchini on a sheet pan.
3. Sprinkle the casserole with paprika, oregano, salt, and black pepper, then drizzle with olive oil.
4. Combine everything and toss until covered completely.
5. Cook for 20 to 25 minutes, or until the veggies are soft and the sausages are browned, in the oven.
6. Serve with a garnish of fresh parsley if desired.

81. Easy Meatloaf

Ingredients:

- 1 ½ lbs ground beef
- One egg
- One onion, diced
- one cup milk
- one cup of dried bread crumbs
- salt and pepper to taste
- ⅓ cup ketchup
- 2 tbsp. brown sugar
- 2 tbsp. prepared mustard

Directions:

1. Preheat the oven to 175 degrees C (350 degrees F). Lightly grease a 9-by-5-inch loaf pan.
2. Combine the ground beef, onion, milk, bread crumbs, and egg in a sizable dish. Pepper and salt to taste. Insert into the loaf container we just prepared.
3. Thoroughly combine the ketchup, brown sugar, and mustard; pour over the meatloaf and equally distribute.
4. Put into the preheated oven and bake for 60 minutes to an hour.

Snacks and Dessert Recipes

82. Chinese Sweet Bun Dough

Ingredients:

- ½ cup white sugar
- 1 cup warm milk (110 degrees F/45 degrees C)
- 1 tbsp. active dry yeast
- 4 cups bread flour
- Two eggs, beaten
- 6 tbsp. vegetable oil
- 2 tsp. salt
- 2 tsp. water
- 1 tsp. Sesame seeds for garnish

Directions:

1. Combine milk and sugar in a sizable mixing dish; stir until sugar is dissolved. After adding the yeast, stir the mixture and let it sit for 10 minutes, or until the milk begins to foam. Add the flour, salt, and most of the beaten eggs; mix well until well-combined. Save about 1 tbsp. Of the egg in a separate small dish for later.
2. The dough should be elastic and smooth after being kneaded for about 10 minutes on a lightly floured surface. A sticky mixture is desired. You can let the dough rise for two to three hours, or until it has doubled in size, by placing it in a large, oiled bowl, covering it with a damp cloth or plastic wrap, and placing it in a warm place.
3. Cover a baking sheet with parchment paper.
4. Remove the dough from the dish and knead it for about a minute to punch it down. Cut the rope of dough into 12 sections of the same size. Roll each piece into a ball, then

flatten each with your fingers into a disc measuring 5 and 6 inches in circumference.

5. Bring the dough edges over the filling and place about 2 tbsp of your preferred bun filling in the center of the dough circle. To seal in the filling, pinch and twist the tip together. Ensure there are no available spaces. Put the filled buns, seam side down, on the parchment paper while you work on the rest of the buns. The filled buns should rise for 30 minutes while covered in plastic wrap.
6. Pre-heat oven to 375 degrees F. (One-hundred-seventy-five degrees Celsius). Brush each bun's top with the egg wash you made with the remaining beaten egg and water, then top each with a few sesame seeds.
7. Bake buns in the preheated oven for 20 to 30 minutes, or until the tops are golden and shiny, rotating the baking pan halfway through baking. Serve hot.

83. Creamy Whipped Feta

Ingredients:

- Eight oz. diced feta cheese
- ¾ cup Greek yogurt
- One clove of garlic, minced
- ½ tsp. lemon zest
- freshly ground black pepper to taste
- 3 tbsp. olive oil, divided
- 1 tbsp. minced oil-packed dried tomatoes
- 1 tbsp. pine nuts
- 1 tbsp. Minced fresh parsley

Directions:

1. Combine the feta cheese, Greek yogurt, garlic, lemon juice, and black pepper in a food processor. To mix, pulse several times. When the dip is smooth and creamy, for about a minute, slowly drizzle in 2 tbsp—of extra virgin olive oil, scraping down the edges of the bowl as necessary.
2. After transferring it to a dish or plate, top the mixture with sun-dried tomatoes, pine nuts, and parsley. Serve after adding the last of the olive oil.

84. Air Fryer Halloumi Cheese

Ingredients:

- 8 oz. halloumi cheese
- 2 tsp. olive oil
- cooking spray

Directions:

1. The oven fryer to 360 degrees Fahrenheit (180 degrees C).
2. Halloumi should be cut into six equal pieces; each piece should be divided into two and dried with paper towels. Apply olive oil all over.
3. Cooking spray should be lightly applied to the air fryer container. Slices of halloumi should not come into contact as they are placed in the basket. If necessary, divide into two batches and cook for 7 to 9 minutes. Overcooking will make them gelatinous, so watch the time. Distribute immediately.

85. Apple Nachos

Ingredients:

- Two apples, sliced
- 1/4 cup peanut butter
- 1/4 cup chocolate chips
- 1/4 cup diced nuts
- 1/4 cup shredded coconut

Instructions:

1. Put the apple slices in a neat row on a big plate.
2. Drizzle the melted peanut butter over the apple segments.
3. Over the top, sprinkle the chocolate chunks, diced nuts, and coconut shavings.
4. Serve right away.

86. Hummus and Veggie Platter

Ingredients:

- 1 cup hummus
- Carrot sticks
- Celery sticks
- Bell pepper strips
- Cucumber slices
- Cherry tomatoes
- Pita bread or crackers

Instructions:

1. On a big platter, arrange the hummus and vegetables.
2. Serve with crackers or pita bread.

87. Roasted Chickpeas

Ingredients:

- One can of chickpeas, drained and rinsed
- 1 tbsp. olive oil
- Salt and black pepper, to taste
- 1 tsp. paprika
- 1/2 tsp. garlic powder

Instructions:

1. Set the oven's temperature to 400°F (200°C).
2. Spread the legumes out on a baking sheet.
3. Add salt, pepper, paprika, garlic powder, and olive oil for seasoning.
4. Combine everything and toss until covered completely.
5. Bake for 20 to 25 minutes, or until golden.
6. Whether hot or cool, serve.

88. Feta-Spinach Puff Pastry Bites

Ingredients:

- Nonstick cooking spray
- One sheet of frozen puff pastry thawed in the refrigerator
- ¾ cup of mayonnaise
- 1 (6 oz.) container of crumbled feta cheese
- ½ cup of freshly grated Parmesan cheese
- 1 (10 oz.) package of frozen diced spinach, thawed and drained
- Two cloves garlic, minced
- ¼ tsp. Ground black pepper

Directions:

1. Turn the oven temperature up to 375 degrees F. (about 360 F). Apply nonstick cooking spray to the cups of a 24-cup mini muffin tray (or two 12-cup mini muffin pans).
2. A rolling tool shapes the cold, thawed puff pastry sheet into a rectangle on a lightly dusted surface. Make 24 pizza-sized (about 2.5 inches) cuts in the dough. In each cup of the mini muffin pan that has been prepared, gently press a piece of puff pastry and prick with a fork.
3. Combine the mayonnaise, feta cheese, Parmesan cheese, spinach, garlic, and pepper in a dish.
4. With care, equally, distribute the feta-spinach mixture into the cups without overfilling them.
5. Bake in the oven for 15 to 16 minutes or until the pastry is puffy and the edges are golden brown.
6. Before moving the bites to a serving plate, let them cool for 5 minutes on a wire rack in the pan.

89. No-Bake Energy Bites

Ingredients:

- 1 cup rolled oats
- 1/2 cup peanut butter
- 1/2 cup honey
- 1/2 cup chocolate chips
- 1/2 cup shredded coconut
- 1 tsp. vanilla extract

Instructions:

1. Rolling oats, peanut butter, honey, chocolate chips, shredded coconut, and vanilla extract should all be combined in a mixing dish.
2. All of the ingredients should be thoroughly mixed.
3. Make bite-sized balls out of the batter.
4. Set the energy morsels in the refrigerator for an hour.
5. Offer chilled.

90. Caprese Skewers

Ingredients:

- Cherry tomatoes
- Fresh mozzarella balls
- Basil leaves
- Balsamic glaze

Instructions:

1. On a stick, skewer a cherry tomato, a ball of fresh mozzarella, and a basil leaf.
2. Continue by using the remaining ingredients.
3. The spears should be covered in balsamic glaze.
4. Offer chilled.

91. Cinnamon Roasted Almonds

Ingredients:

- 2 cups raw almonds
- 2 tbsp. honey
- 1 tbsp. olive oil
- 1 tsp. ground cinnamon
- 1/2 tsp. salt

Instructions:

1. Set a baking tray on the counter and preheat the oven to 350°F (180°C).
2. It's best to combine the almonds, honey, olive oil, cinnamon, and salt in a single bowl.
3. Everything should be thoroughly combined before adding the nuts.
4. In a preheated oven, spread the mixture out on the prepared baking sheet and bake for 10–15 minutes.
5. Prior to serving, let the food fully cool.

92. Homemade Trail Mix

Ingredients:

- 1 cup almonds
- 1 cup cashews
- 1 cup dried cranberries
- 1 cup dark chocolate chips

Instructions:

1. Almonds, cashews, dried cranberries, and dark chocolate chips should all be combined in a mixing dish.
2. Mix each ingredient thoroughly to ensure even distribution.
3. When a snack is required, give it in an airtight container.

93. Pizza Sliders

Ingredients:

- cooking spray
- 1 ½ cups (6 oz.) finely pre-shredded low-moisture part-skim mozzarella cheese
- One cup (about 3 1/2 oz.) finely pre-shredded Italian cheese blend
- ¼ cup finely diced fresh basil
- ¼ tsp. black pepper
- 2 tsp. dried Italian seasoning, divided
- One ⅓ cups pizza sauce (from 1 [13-oz.] jar)
- 2 tbsp. sun-dried tomato pesto
- 1 (12 counts) package Hawaiian sweet rolls
- ¾ cup (about three oz.) thinly sliced pepperoni
- 2 tbsp. unsalted butter
- 1 tbsp. Grated Parmesan cheese
- ¾ tsp. garlic powder

Directions:

1. Turn the oven temperature up to 375 degrees F. (190 degrees F). A baking sheet lined with parchment paper should be placed on top of a cooling rack with a rim. Spray some frying oil on the rack.
2. Combine mozzarella, an Italian cheese mixture, basil, pepper, and 1 1/2 tsp. of Italian seasoning in a small dish. Place away.
3. In another small dish, combine the pesto and pizza sauce. Place away.

4. Without separating the individual rolls from the slab, cut the slab in half horizontally with a serrated knife. Rolls should be arranged in a bottom layer on the baking tray. Set the top layer of rolls away.
5. Half of the cheese combination should be evenly distributed over the bottom layer of rolls before the pepperoni and sauce are distributed equally on top. Layers once more.
6. About 15 minutes should pass in the prepared oven as the cheese melts.
7. Meanwhile, mix the remaining half a teaspoon. of Italian seasoning, the Parmesan, and the butter in a small saucepan. To melt the butter, cook for 1 to 2 minutes over medium heat, stirring occasionally. Set aside.
8. Rolls should be removed from the oven, topped with more rolls, and then equally brushed with the butter mixture. Please return to the oven and roast the rolls for another five minutes or until they are crisp and golden brown. Serve the pastries separately and right away.

94. Greek Yogurt Dip with Veggies

Ingredients:

- 1 cup Greek yogurt
- 1/4 cup diced fresh dill
- 1 tbsp. lemon juice
- 1/2 tsp. garlic powder
- Salt and black pepper, to taste
- Assorted veggies for dipping (e.g., carrots, cucumbers, bell peppers)

Instructions:

1. Greek yogurt, dill, lemon juice, garlic powder, salt, and black pepper should all be combined in a mixing dish.
2. All of the ingredients should be thoroughly mixed.
3. Serve alongside the mixed vegetables for marinating.

95. Avocado Toast

Ingredients:

- Two slices whole grain bread
- One ripe avocado
- Salt and black pepper, to taste
- Optional toppings: cherry tomatoes, sliced radishes, crumbled feta cheese

Instructions:

1. Toasted bread should be as crunchy as you like it.
2. In a small mixing dish, mash the avocado and season with salt and black pepper.
3. The toast is covered in pureed avocado.
4. Serve after adding any preferred garnishes.

96. Antipasto Skewers

Ingredients:

- Cherry tomatoes Mozzarella balls
- Slices of salami or prosciutto
- Marinated artichoke hearts
- Olives
- Toothpicks

Instructions:

1. Put a toothpick in each: a cherry tomato, a mozzarella ball, a slice of salami or prosciutto, an artichoke center, and an olive.
2. Continue by using the remaining ingredients.
3. Offer chilled.

97. Chocolate Fudge Brownies

Ingredients:

- 1 cup all-purpose flour
- 3/4 cup cocoa powder
- 1/2 tsp. salt
- 1/2 tsp. baking powder
- 1 cup unsalted butter, melted
- 2 cups granulated sugar
- Four large eggs
- 2 tsp. vanilla extract
- 1 cup semisweet chocolate chips

Instructions:

1. Grease a 9x13 inch baking sheet and preheat the oven to 350°F (175°C).
2. In a large mixing bowl, whisk together the flour, baking soda, salt, and cocoa powder.
3. In a separate bowl, thoroughly combine the melted butter and granulated sugar.
4. The butter mixture will be smoother after adding the eggs and vanilla essence.
5. Mix until combined after gradually incorporating the dry ingredients into the wet components.
6. Add the chocolate chunks and stir.
7. Bake for 25-30 minutes, or until a toothpick inserted in the center comes out clean, after you've poured the batter into the prepared pan.
8. Before slicing and serving, let the brownies cool fully.

98. Rough Puff

Ingredients:

- two cups all-purpose flour, plus more for dusting
- ½ tsp. kosher salt
- 1 cup cold unsalted butter, cubed
- ½ cup cold water

Directions:

1. Combine the flour and salt in the bowl of a stand mixer with a paddle tool. Add butter and stir with your fingers until the flour is evenly coated.
2. Fill a basin with water. For about 45 seconds, on medium speed, mix the dough until it resembles a shaggy mass.
3. Refrigerate for about 20 minutes, or until butter is firm but not brittle, after covering the dish with plastic wrap.
4. Sprinkle your work surface with flour and roll the dough into a rectangle about 10 1/2 by 6 inches and 1/2 an inch thick.
5. The center third of the dough is folded over the lengthier side's first third. Fold the last third over to the center. (like a letter) Folded in half lengthwise. After folding the dough, wrap it tightly in plastic wrap and chill it for 30 minutes. Continue folding, rolling, and chilling the dough four more times, rotating it 90 degrees before rolling.
6. Once you've completed the final fold, wrap the dough tightly in plastic and place it in the fridge for at least an hour and up to two days.

99. Classic Chocolate Chip Cookies

Ingredients:

- 2 1/4 cups all-purpose flour
- 1 tsp. baking soda
- 1 tsp. salt
- 1 cup unsalted butter, softened
- 3/4 cup granulated sugar
- 3/4 cup brown sugar
- Two large eggs
- 2 tsp. vanilla extract
- 2 cups semisweet chocolate chips

Instructions:

1. Prepare an oven rack and prepare the oven to 375 degrees Fahrenheit (190 degrees Celsius).
2. Combine the flour, baking powder, and salt in a large bowl.
3. Softened butter, granulated sugar, and brown sugar should be creamed until light and fluffy in a separate mixing dish.
4. The butter mixture will be smoother after the addition of the eggs and vanilla essence.
5. Mix until just combined after gradually incorporating the dry ingredients into the wet components.
6. Add the chocolate chunks and stir.
7. Put cookie dough by the spoonful onto the baking sheet and bake for 10 to 12 minutes, or until the edges are golden.
8. After a couple of minutes, transfer the cookies to a wire rack to finish cooling.

100. Chocolate Chip Cookies

Ingredients:

- one cup (2 sticks) of unsalted butter at room temperature
- 1 cup white sugar
- 1 cup brown sugar
- Two large eggs
- 1 tsp. vanilla extract
- 2 1/4 cups all-purpose flour
- 1 tsp. baking soda
- 1 tsp. salt
- 2 cups semisweet chocolate chips

Instructions:

1. Set a baking tray on the counter and preheat the oven to 375°F (190°C).
2. Butter, white, and brown sugar should be thoroughly combined in a mixing dish until light and fluffy.
3. After blending, add eggs and vanilla extract.
4. Separately, blend the dry ingredients (flour, baking powder, and salt).
5. Blend the dry components thoroughly after gradually incorporating them into the butter mixture.
6. Add the chocolate chunks and stir.
7. On the prepared baking tray, drop tbsp—Bake the dough for 10 to 12 minutes or until golden brown.
8. Cool before placing on a wire rack.

101. Strawberry Shortcake

Ingredients:

- 1 quart fresh strawberries, hulled and sliced
- 1/2 cup white sugar
- 2 cups all-purpose flour
- 1 tbsp. baking powder
- 1/4 tsp. salt
- 1/4 cup unsalted butter, at room temperature
- 1 cup whole milk
- Whipped cream for serving

Instructions:

1. The oven should be heated to 425°F (218°C).
2. Strawberries and sugar should be mixed together in a bowl. Reserve after a thorough stirring.
3. In a separate bowl, mix the dry ingredients (flour, salt, baking soda).
4. Mix in the butter until the texture resembles coarse crumbs.
5. Stir in the milk gradually until a soft dough develops.
6. Put spoonfuls of the dough onto a baking pan that has been greased.
7. Cook for 12 to 15 minutes, or until a deep, golden brown.
8. Shortcakes should be cut in two, then the strawberry filling and whipped cream should be placed inside.

102. Chocolate Mousse

Ingredients:

- 1 cup semisweet chocolate chips
- 1/4 cup unsalted butter
- Three large eggs separated
- 1/4 cup white sugar
- 1/2 cup heavy cream

Instructions:

1. Butter and chocolate chunks should be melted in a double boiler or a heatproof bowl set over a pot of simmering water. Do it frequently.
2. Remove from the fire and give it a little time to cool.
3. Egg whites should be beaten until stiff peaks form.
4. It's essential to beat egg whites until firm peaks form.
5. Toss the egg yolk combined with the melted chocolate.
6. After beating the egg whites, fold them into the chocolate concoction.
7. Beat the heavy cream until soft peaks appear in a different mixing bowl.
8. Whip the milk and incorporate it into the chocolate mixture.
9. Put the mousse in serving bowls or plates and refrigerate for at least two hours before serving.

103. Peanut Butter M&M Cookies

Ingredients:

- 1 cup creamy peanut butter
- ¾ cup firmly packed brown sugar
- 2 tbsp. firmly packed brown sugar
- One large egg at room temperature
- 1 tsp. baking soda
- 1 ½ tsp. vanilla extract
- ¼ tsp. salt
- ⅛ tsp. ground nutmeg
- ½ cup mini candy-coated chocolate pieces (such as mini M&M's®)

Directions:

1. Get the oven to a temperature of 350 degrees F. 175 degrees C.. Using parchment paper, line two baking pans.
2. Egg, baking soda, vanilla, salt, nutmeg, and 3/4 cup plus 2 tsp. Brown sugar is all mixed. Add the tiny chocolate M&Ms.
3. Scoop out dough spheres that are 1 1/2 tbsp. In size and space them 1 inch apart on the baking sheets. Flatten balls of dough to a thickness of about an inch and a half.
4. About 10 minutes into baking, the tops of the biscuits should start to crack slightly. Before transferring the cookies to a wire rack to finish cooling, give them 10 minutes to cool on the baking sheets.

104. Peanut Butter Whipped Cream

Ingredients:

- 2 cups heavy whipping cream
- 1 cup powdered sugar
- ⅓ cup creamy peanut butter
- ½ tsp. vanilla extract

Directions:

1. Mix the cream, sugar, peanut butter, and vanilla essence in a bowl.
2. For one to two minutes, using a high-speed electric mixer, whip the mixture until stiff peaks form.
3. Place in the fridge to store.

105. Best Mud Pie

Ingredients:

- 1 (6 oz.) chocolate sandwich cookie crumb crust
- 1-quart coffee ice cream, divided
- 1 (12 oz.) package of miniature chocolate chips
- 1 (12 oz.) jar of hot fudge topping
- ½ (18 oz.) package of crushed chocolate sandwich cookies divided
- 1 (8 oz.) container of frozen whipped topping, thawed
- ¾ cup chocolate syrup

Directions:

1. For about 30 minutes, freeze the crust until it is solid.
2. Half the coffee ice cream should be placed in a dish and softened for 10 minutes. Restore the ice cream that is left. Mini chocolate chunks and softened ice cream should be combined. Over the frozen crust, evenly spread the concoction. For two hours, cover in plastic wrap and freeze.
3. The fudge topping needs only 30 seconds in the microwave on low to become pourable. Put some in a dish. The leftover cookie crumbs are mixed into the fudge topping after 2 tbsp. Are set away for garnish.
4. The pie should be removed from the fridge and covered with the fudge mixture and ice cream. For two hours, cover in plastic wrap and put back in the freezer.
5. Take any leftover coffee ice cream out of the freezer and set it at room temperature for ten minutes. Over the chocolate layer, spread ice cream. Cover with plastic wrap for an additional two hours and place back in the fridge.

6. After removing the pie, cover it with whipped cream. To garnish, add the cookie bits you saved. Cover with plastic wrap and chill for another 2 hours.
7. Slice the pie into serving-sized portions and drizzle 1 tbsp of chocolate syrup over each portion.

106. TikTok Brownies

Ingredients:

- ½ cup unsalted butter, plus additional for greasing pan
- ⅓ cup cocoa powder
- one cup of granulated sugar
- 2 tsp. vanilla extract
- Two large eggs
- ½ cup all-purpose flour

Directions:

1. Prepare oven to bake at 350 degrees Fahrenheit. (175 degrees C). Prepare a square, 8- inch metal baking dish by greasing it thoroughly.
2. In a sizable pot set over low heat, melt the butter. Please turn off the heat and allow it to settle for five minutes. Add vanilla essence, sugar, and cocoa powder by whisking. Put in the eggs one by one and mix them in. It's time to add the flour and give it a quick stir. Smooth the surface after scraping the mixture into the prepared pan.
3. For twenty to twenty-five minutes in the preheated oven or until a toothpick stuck in the center comes out clean.
4. Wait at least 45 minutes after taking it out of the oven before slicing it.

107. Ruffled Milk Pie

Ingredients:

- 12 tbsp. Melted Ghee or clarified butter, divided
- ¾ cup granulated sugar
- ½ tsp. ground cinnamon
- ⅛ tsp. table salt
- 14 sheets of frozen phyllo dough, thawed
- 1 ¼ cups whole milk
- ¼ cup heavy cream
- Five large eggs
- 1 tsp. vanilla extract
- 1 tbsp. powdered sugar

Directions:

1. Set oven to 375 degrees Fahrenheit. (190 degrees C). One tbsp. of butter should be brushed around a nine-1/2-inch deep dish pie pan.
2. Combine the sugar, cinnamon, and salt in a small bowl.
3. Butter one side of one sheet of phyllo dough after placing it on a cutting board or clean work area. Push the short edges of the phyllo towards one another to form a rope, then carefully scrunch it up.
4. Place in the center of the baking dish that has been prepped after loosely coiling. Repeat with the remaining phyllo sheets and butter, packing them firmly into a concentric circle around the central coil.
5. Two tsp. of the spiced sugar mixture should be scattered on top.

6. For about 25 minutes, bake in the preheated oven until brown. Remove from oven, then lower heat to 325 degrees F (165 degrees C).
7. While the phyllo is baking, heat the milk and cream in a small saucepan over medium heat until they are almost at a boil. Get rid of the humidity.
8. Whisk together the eggs, vanilla, and leftover spiced sugar mixture in a dish. Add the hot milk slowly while continuing to whisk until well combined. Return the baking tray with the phyllo to the oven after immediately pouring spiced milk over it.
9. Custard should only be baked for 20–25 minutes. Sprinkle with icing sugar. At room temperature or tepid, serve.

108. Brownie Pie

Ingredients:

Crust:

- One ¼ cup all-purpose flour, plus more for rolling
- 1 tbsp. granulated sugar
- ½ tsp. kosher salt
- ½ cup cold unsalted butter cut into 1/2-inch pieces
- 3 tbsp. Ice water, or more as needed

Filling:

- 10 tbsp. unsalted butter melted and cooled
- ¾ cup granulated sugar
- Two large eggs at room temperature
- One large egg yolk at room temperature
- 2 tbsp. canola oil
- 1 tsp. vanilla extract
- ¾ cup unsweetened cocoa powder
- ½ cup all-purpose flour
- 2 tsp. Instant espresso granules
- ½ tsp. kosher salt
- ½ cup diced walnuts or hazelnuts
- ½ cup semisweet chocolate chips, divided

Directions:

1. Pulse the ingredients for the crust three times in a food processor to incorporate the flour, sugar, and tsp. using salt. In a food processor, combine the flour and cold butter. Till butter resembles pea-sized chunks, pulse about six

times. Put 3 tsp. of water on top of the butter mixture. The dough should form beads that resemble couscous after about six pulses. If necessary, add one more spoonful of ice water.

2. Press the dough into a single mass after transferring it to a work area. The dough should be formed and pressed into a disc.
3. Wrap in plastic and store in the fridge for up to two days.
4. The dough should be unwrapped and placed in a work area lightly dusted with flour. Give the dough 10 minutes to relax at room temperature. Flour the dough's upper surface. Roll the disc into a 12-inch circle with a rolling pin that has been gently dusted with flour.
5. A 9-inch pie dish, inserted into the bottom and up the sides. To crimp the ends, fold them under as desired. Freeze, wrapped in plastic, for 30 minutes.
6. Get the oven to a temperature of 350 degrees F. 175 degrees C. After placing parchment paper over the dough, fill the pie dish with dried beans or pie weights.
7. For a crisp exterior, bake for 15 minutes in an oven preheated to 400 degrees.
8. Carefully take out of the oven the pie plate, baking paper, and pie weights. Put the dish in the oven for 8-12 minutes, or until the crust is golden.
9. Place on a wire tray and refrigerate for 20 minutes or until cold.
10. Melted butter, sugar, eggs, egg yolk, canola oil, and vanilla essence should all be thoroughly combined and smooth in a bowl. Just mix the cocoa, flour, instant espresso, and salt. Add nuts and 1/4 cup of chocolate chunks and mix well.

11. Put the ingredients into the prepared crust and use a small offset spatula to level the surface. Top the pie with the leftover 1/4 cup of chocolate chips.
12. If using a toothpick to check doneness, bake for 30–35 minutes. If the pie crust is browning too quickly, tent it with aluminum foil. Wait 20 minutes before serving.

109. Spanish Flan

Ingredients:

- 1 cup white sugar
- 3 large eggs
- one (14 oz.) can of sweetened condensed milk
- 1 (12 fluid oz.) can evaporate milk
- 1 tbsp. vanilla extract

Directions:

1. Get the oven to a temperature of 350 degrees F. 175 degrees C..
2. Melt the sugar in a medium saucepan over low heat until it turns golden. Carefully pour hot syrup into a round glass baking dish, turn the dish so that the bottom and sides are coated evenly, and then set aside.
3. In a large dish, beat the eggs. Beat in the condensed, evaporated, and vanilla after adding them. Fill the baking dish with the egg mixture and top with foil.
4. Toss into a hot oven and leave for an hour. Cool down completely.
5. To serve, carefully invert the flan onto a serving dish with a rim and drizzle the caramel sauce over the top.

110. Frosty Strawberry Squares

Ingredients:

- 1 cup all-purpose flour
- ½ cup packed brown sugar
- ½ cup diced walnuts
- ½ cup melted butter
- Two egg whites
- 1 cup white sugar
- 2 cups sliced strawberries
- 2 tbsp. lemon juice
- 1 cup heavy cream

Directions:

1. Get the oven to a temperature of 350 degrees F. 175 degrees C.. A 9x13-inch pastry pan should be greased.
2. A baking pan with a rim should be lined with foil. It's best to mix the flour, sugar, nuts, and melted butter in one dish. About 15 minutes of oven toasting time should result in fragrant walnuts; turn frequently. The bottom of the 9x13-inch dish should be equally covered with 2/3 of the walnut mixture.
3. In a large bowl, whip the egg whites and lemon juice until soft peaks form. Whip the white sugar in gradually while maintaining solid peaks. Strawberries are folded in.
4. In a separate bowl, use an electric mixer to whip the cream until it is stiff but not grainy. Add to the strawberry concoction by folding. Spread equally with a spoon over the dish's crust. Add the leftover walnut mixture on top. Overnight or for six hours, freeze.

111. Banana Cream Pie

Ingredients:

- ¾ cup white sugar
- ⅓ cup all-purpose flour
- ¼ tsp. salt
- 2 cups milk
- Three egg yolks, beaten
- 2 tbsp. butter
- 1 ¼ tsp. vanilla extract
- 1 (9-inch) baked pastry shell, cooled
- Four bananas, sliced

Directions:

1. Get the oven to a temperature of 350 degrees F. 175 degrees C..
2. In a pot, mix salt, flour, and sugar. Stir in milk gradually. Cook over medium heat while continuously stirring until the mixture boils and thickens. After two more minutes of cooking and stirring, turn off the heat.
3. Whisk a small quantity of the hot milk mixture into the egg yolks in a medium bowl until they are smooth. Then, gradually whisk the egg yolk mixture into the saucepan. For an additional 2 minutes, cook with continuous stirring over medium-low heat. Add vanilla and butter after removing from the flame.
4. Fill the pastry shell with sliced bananas, then top with the pudding mixture.
5. To ensure the center is set, bake for 12–15 minutes. Please wait an hour to serve dessert after chilling it in the fridge.

Smoothies Recipes

112. Strawberry Banana Smoothie

Ingredients:

- One banana, sliced
- 1 cup of frozen strawberries
- 1/2 cup of plain Greek yogurt
- 1/2 cup of almond milk
- 1 tbsp. of honey

Instructions:

1. Blend all components in a blender until they are entirely smooth.
2. More almond milk can be added if the shake is too thick.
3. Pour into a glass and enjoy..

113. Mango Lassi Smoothie

Ingredients:

- 1 cup of diced mango
- 1/2 cup of plain Greek yogurt
- 1/2 cup of milk
- 1 tbsp. of honey
- 1/4 tsp. of ground cardamom
- 1/4 tsp. of vanilla extract

Instructions:

1. Blend all components in a blender until they are entirely smooth.
2. Pour into a glass and enjoy..

114. Blueberry Kale Smoothie

Ingredients:

- 1 cup of frozen blueberries
- 1 cup of kale leaves, stems removed
- 1/2 banana, sliced
- 1/2 cup of plain Greek yogurt
- 1/2 cup of almond milk
- 1 tbsp. of honey

Instructions:

1. Blend all components in a blender until they are entirely smooth.
2. More almond milk can be added if the shake is too thick.
3. Pour into a glass and enjoy..

115. Orange Creamsicle Smoothie

Ingredients:

- 1 cup of orange juice
- 1/2 cup of vanilla Greek yogurt
- 1/2 cup of ice cubes
- 1/2 tsp. of vanilla extract
- 1 tbsp. of honey

Instructions:

1. Blend all components in a blender until they are entirely smooth.
2. Add milk or more orange juice if the drink is too thick.
3. Pour into a glass and enjoy..

116. Mixed Berry Smoothie

Ingredients:

- 1/2 cup of frozen mixed berries
- 1/2 banana, sliced
- 1/2 cup of plain Greek yogurt
- 1/2 cup of almond milk
- 1 tbsp. of honey

Instructions:

1. Blend all components in a blender until they are entirely smooth.
2. More almond milk can be added if the shake is too thick.
3. Pour into a glass and enjoy..

117. Chocolate Raspberry Smoothie

Ingredients:

- 1/2 cup of frozen raspberries
- One banana, sliced
- 1 tbsp. of cocoa powder
- 1/2 cup of plain Greek yogurt
- 1/2 cup of almond milk
- 1 tbsp. of honey

Instructions:

1. Blend all components in a blender until they are entirely smooth.
2. More almond milk can be added if the shake is too thick.
3. Pour into a glass and enjoy..

118. Apple Cinnamon Smoothie

Ingredients:

- One apple, peeled and sliced
- 1/2 banana, sliced
- 1/2 cup of plain Greek yogurt
- 1/2 cup of almond milk
- 1/2 tsp. of cinnamon
- 1 tbsp. of honey

Instructions:

1. Blend all components in a blender until they are entirely smooth.
2. More almond milk can be added if the shake is too thick.
3. Pour into a glass and enjoy..

119. Tropical Mango Pineapple Smoothie

Ingredients:

- 1 cup of frozen mango chunks
- 1/2 cup of frozen pineapple chunks
- One banana, sliced
- 1/2 cup of coconut milk
- 1/2 cup of orange juice
- 1 tbsp. of honey

Instructions:

1. Blend all components in a blender until they are entirely smooth.
2. If the drink is too thick, feel free to add more coconut milk or orange juice.
3. Pour into a glass and enjoy.

120. Carrot Ginger Smoothie

Ingredients:

- Two carrots, peeled and sliced
- One apple, peeled and sliced
- 1/2 inch piece of fresh ginger, peeled and grated
- 1/2 cup of plain Greek yogurt
- 1/2 cup of almond milk
- 1 tbsp. of honey

Instructions:

1. Blend all components in a blender until they are entirely smooth.
2. More almond milk can be added if the shake is too thick.
3. Pour into a glass and enjoy..

121. Watermelon Mint Smoothie

Ingredients:

- 2 cups of cubed watermelon
- 1/2 cup of plain Greek yogurt
- 1/4 cup of fresh mint leaves
- 1 tbsp. of honey
- 1/2 cup of ice cubes

Instructions:

1. Blend all components in a blender until they are entirely smooth.
2. Add more water or ice chunks to the smoothie if it is too thick.
3. Pour into a glass and enjoy.

122. Strawberry Kiwi Smoothie

Ingredients:

- 1 cup of frozen strawberries
- One kiwi, peeled and sliced
- 1/2 cup of plain Greek yogurt
- 1/2 cup of orange juice
- 1 tbsp. of honey

Instructions:

1. Blend all components in a blender until they are entirely smooth.
2. More orange juice should be added if the drink is too thick.
3. Put some in a tumbler and sip it.

123. Avocado Banana Smoothie

Ingredients:

- One banana, sliced
- 1/2 avocado, peeled and pitted
- 1/2 cup of almond milk
- 1/2 cup of plain Greek yogurt
- 1 tbsp. of honey
- 1/2 cup of ice cubes

Instructions:

1. Blend all components in a blender until they are entirely smooth.
2. Add more ice or almond milk if the drink is too thick.
3. Pour into a glass and enjoy.

124. Chocolate Cherry Smoothie

Ingredients:

- 1 cup of frozen cherries
- 1/2 banana, sliced
- 1 tbsp. of cocoa powder
- 1/2 cup of plain Greek yogurt
- 1/2 cup of almond milk
- 1 tbsp. of honey
- 1/2 cup of ice cubes

Instructions:

1. Blend all components in a blender until they are entirely smooth.
2. Add more ice or almond milk if the drink is too thick.
3. Pour into a glass and enjoy..

125. Blackberry Vanilla Smoothie

Ingredients:

- 1 cup of frozen blackberries
- 1/2 cup of plain Greek yogurt
- 1/2 cup of almond milk
- 1 tsp. of vanilla extract
- 1 tbsp. of honey
- 1/2 cup of ice cubes

Instructions:

1. Blend all items in a blender until completely smooth.
2. Add more almond milk or ice chunks if the smoothie is too thick.
3. Pour into a tumbler, then sip.

126. Peach Melba Smoothie

Ingredients:

- One peach, pitted and sliced
- 1 cup of frozen raspberries
- 1/2 cup of plain Greek yogurt
- 1/2 cup of almond milk
- 1 tbsp. of honey
- 1/2 cup of ice cubes

Instructions:

1. Blend all components in a blender until they are entirely smooth.
2. Add more ice or almond milk if the drink is too thick.
3. Pour into a glass and enjoy..

127. Spinach Pineapple Smoothie

Ingredients:

- 2 cups of fresh spinach
- 1 cup of frozen pineapple chunks
- 1/2 banana, sliced
- 1/2 cup of plain Greek yogurt
- 1/2 cup of coconut milk
- 1 tbsp. of honey
- 1/2 cup of ice cubes

Instructions:

1. Blend all components in a blender until they are entirely smooth.
2. The thickness of the smoothie can be adjusted by adding more coconut milk or ice.
3. Pour into a glass and enjoy.

128. Coffee Protein Smoothie

Ingredients:

- One banana, sliced
- One scoop of chocolate protein powder
- 1/2 cup of cold coffee
- 1/2 cup of almond milk
- 1 tbsp. of cocoa powder
- 1/2 cup of ice cubes

Instructions:

1. Blend all components in a blender until they are entirely smooth.
2. Add more ice or almond milk if the drink is too thick.
3. Pour into a glass and enjoy.

129. Mango Green Tea Smoothie

Ingredients:

- 1 cup of brewed green tea, chilled
- 1 cup of frozen mango chunks
- 1/2 banana, sliced
- 1/2 cup of plain Greek yogurt
- 1 tbsp. of honey
- 1/2 cup of ice cubes

Instructions:

1. Blend all components in a blender until they are entirely smooth.
2. If the consistency of the smoothie is off, try adding some more ice or green tea.
3. Pour into a glass and enjoy.

130. Blueberry Muffin Smoothie

Ingredients:

- 1 cup of frozen blueberries
- 1/2 banana, sliced
- 1/2 cup of plain Greek yogurt
- 1/2 cup of almond milk
- 1 tbsp. of honey
- 1/2 tsp. of vanilla extract
- 1/4 tsp. of cinnamon
- 1/2 cup of ice cubes

Instructions:

1. Blend all components in a blender until they are entirely smooth.
2. Add more ice or almond milk if the drink is too thick.
3. Pour into a glass and enjoy.

131. Honeydew Lime Smoothie

Ingredients:

- 1 cup of honeydew melon, cubed
- 1/2 banana, sliced
- 1/2 cup of plain Greek yogurt
- 1/2 cup of coconut water
- 1 tbsp. of honey
- 1/2 lime, juiced
- 1/2 cup of ice cubes

Instructions:

1. Blend all components in a blender until they are entirely smooth.
2. If the smoothie is too thick, add more coconut water or ice cubes.
3. Pour into a glass and enjoy.

132. Beetroot Berry Smoothie

Ingredients:

- One small cooked beetroot, diced
- 1 cup of frozen mixed berries
- 1/2 banana, sliced
- 1/2 cup of plain Greek yogurt
- 1/2 cup of almond milk
- 1 tbsp. of honey
- 1/2 tsp. of vanilla extract
- 1/2 cup of ice cubes

Instructions:

1. Blend all components in a blender until they are entirely smooth.
2. Add more ice or almond milk if the drink is too thick.
3. Pour into a glass and enjoy..

133. Cherry Vanilla Smoothie

Ingredients:

- 1 cup of frozen cherries
- 1/2 banana, sliced
- 1/2 cup of plain Greek yogurt
- 1/2 cup of almond milk
- 1 tbsp. of honey
- 1/2 tsp. of vanilla extract
- 1/2 cup of ice cubes

Instructions:

1. Blend all components in a blender until they are entirely smooth.
2. Add more ice or almond milk if the drink is too thick.
3. Pour into a glass and enjoy.

134. Pina Colada Smoothie

Ingredients:

- 1 cup of frozen pineapple chunks
- 1/2 banana, sliced
- 1/2 cup of plain Greek yogurt
- 1/2 cup of coconut milk
- 1 tbsp. of honey
- 1/2 tsp. of vanilla extract
- 1/2 cup of ice cubes

Instructions:

1. Blend all components in a blender until they are entirely smooth.
2. The thickness of the smoothie can be adjusted by adding more coconut milk or ice.
3. Pour into a glass and enjoy.

Conclusion

In conclusion, The Cirrhosis Cookbook is an excellent resource for individuals with cirrhosis who want to manage their condition through diet. The cookbook provides a wealth of information on the best foods to eat and avoid for cirrhosis patients and a wide range of delicious and nutritious recipes to try. By following the guidelines and recipes in this cookbook, individuals with cirrhosis can improve their overall health and quality of life while enjoying tasty and satisfying meals. It is important to note that the cookbook should be used with medical advice from a healthcare professional to ensure that dietary needs are met, and individual health goals are achieved. Overall, The Cirrhosis Cookbook is a valuable tool for anyone with cirrhosis who wants to take control of their health and well-being through healthy eating.

www.ingramcontent.com/pod-product-compliance
Lightning Source LLC
LaVergne TN
LVHW010104170826
845678LV00012B/2242